BREAK THROUGH

TO YOUR

BREAKTHROUGH

Scriptures are taken from the Amplified Bible.

Publisher's Cataloging in Publication

Shiloh Esq., Brandy D.

ISBN-13: 978-1984335623

ISBN-10: 1984335626

Book formatted and designed by:

CSJ Media Publishing

www.csjmediapublishing.com

BREAK THROUGH

TO YOUR

BREAKTHROUGH

You Are Destined For Greatness

Brandy D. Shiloh, Esq.

CONTENTS

DEDICATION

This Book is dedicated to my Heavenly Father. From whom all things are given and to whom I shall return all things. Thank you Father for the gift of life, love, and your Son, my Lord and Savior Jesus Christ. I Live For You!

To my Mother, you are, have always been, and will always be a source of my inspiration . . . the Apple of my eye.

To my "Iron", Proverbs 27:17. I thank God for the gift of you. So let's go out and expand the Kingdom of God, like He called us to do.

To my Pastors, a structure is only as strong as the foundation it is built upon. Thank you for laying the strong spiritual foundation that served as part of the impetus behind my spiritual growth and this particular journey of <u>Break Through To Your Breakthrough</u>.

MY TESTIMONY

How It Came To Be

Many folks write books after having gone through trials or tragedy, lived it, conquered it, overcome it, and decided to tell a story about it. Then that story translates into a book to help or entertain others. While I think that is a great way to inspire people and helpful to the author as well, that is not my testimony (at least not for this book). Like those other writers, I was really hoping to be able to share my story with you after having overcome the current challenges I am facing.

However, I can honestly tell you that is not where I am at this point and not what I am writing about in this literary work. Rather where I am is right in the midst of a storm, and right now at this very moment, I have not yet been able to pull myself out.

So instead of waiting until I am completely out of the storm to share with you how I overcame it and show you how to do the same, I have decided to write through the storm. And in doing so, I will share with you how I am relying on God to help me out of it every step of the way.

With every word that I type, I sincerely believe that God will help deliver me out of the financial, the physical, and the personal struggles I am currently going through. And as He does, everything that I go through and deal with through the next several months, you will go through with me.

You will experience my experiences as you read and as I live through them minute by minute. It is probably a little risky, but I am willing and committed to what I believe God has asked me to do. I trust that God will help you break through your struggles as you read about mine.

This book is about Breakthrough, mine and yours. A breakthrough can be defined as overcoming an obstacle or restriction, and as you remove the obstacle, you are able to experience achievement and success in your life that paves the way for further progress. Our Breakthrough is exactly what we want and need in our lives in order to fully experience the awesome life God has planned for us.

Essentially, I am expecting a breakthrough in my life while writing this book about how you can get a breakthrough in your life. Why this approach, you ask? Because this is the direction that God has led me. This is what He has asked me to do to obtain my breakthrough. It is a demonstration of faith and trust in Him. And as I demonstrate that faith and trust in

Him, I want to show you that He can not only do this for me but also prove that He can do this for you too.

I am trusting God each step of the way. In fact, a true and concrete demonstration of my faith and my trust in the Word of God is writing this without having been delivered from the state that I am in. Okay, okay, in the event you don't quite understand what I am saying here, what I am attempting to express to you is that I am writing about faith and hope while I am actually learning to hold on to my faith and hope. I am in the midst of trying to break strongholds as I write to you about breaking strongholds.

I am not sharing this to show you how special or unique I am. I am you! I too am looking for my life to change. I am looking to break free from those things that are preventing me from a breakthrough in my life so that I can break through to the next level. I too am merely an imperfect person, young in faith, believing, hoping, and praying for victory over the challenges of life. I am looking to be strong enough to withstand what this world brings us.

This book isn't about how I have it all figured out and how I'm living the best years of my life or even about how you will live the best years of your life if you read this, but just the opposite. As you continue to read, you will hear just how many mistakes I have made and how many times I have fallen.

But thank God that we are not measured by how many times we have fallen but by how many times we have gotten ourselves up, dusted ourselves off, and believed God for the strength to stay in the fight. And it is my humble prayer that you will have the opportunity to learn by watching how many times I have fallen yet be encouraged through how many times I have gotten up.

When I first started writing this book, I was heading in a totally different direction. Initially I only wanted to focus on the state of the economy and the gloomy news constantly on television, radio, and newspapers that seemed to find a way to seep into our spirits, filling people with doubt, insecurity, and fear.

And while the principles outlined in this book are certainly applicable to pulling you (us) out of financial despair, it is also a vehicle to encourage you and help pull you out of any other circumstance you might be facing as well. It is a tool for encouraging, empowering, restoring, reverberating, renewing, reviving, and regenerating the spirits, the hearts, and the souls of all who dare to read this book.

To whom much is given, much is required. (Luke 12:48) And if you are in the midst of challenging times, if you are facing trial after trial after trial and if you find that your best effort is being outweighed by the hard times you are facing, just know this, you are destined for greatness! That means that God has something spectacular in store for you.

If you are getting hit in the place where it hurts the most, just know that He is strengthening you for a Herculean task that will bring forth a breakthrough in your life. He is preparing you for absolute greatness. It means that He is calling you to better, bigger, deeper things. And through it, He is calling you into a closer, more intimate relationship with Him.

I mean if you think about it simplistically, we all face the challenges that we face because (1) God wants us to rely on Him versus us relying on ourselves all the time, (2) God is toughening us up for what's to come and wants to make sure we are prepared, and (3) it means that after we have relied on Him, after we have toughened up and closed the gap of weakness in that area of our lives, God has something totally awesome waiting for us—blessing beyond blessing.

So what are you planning to do? Do you believe these reasons as to why you are going through challenging times, or do you just weather the storm, let it pass, and move on? And if that's you, then I understand. As the scripture says, "Many are called but few are chosen" (Mathew 22:14).

You may have been called, but because you did not heed the response or answer the call, you were not chosen.

Don't let this be you. Answer the call, and if you think you are not quite ready to answer the call but have slid back or fallen down, then at least get up, dust yourself off, and keep moving. Your Breakthrough Awaits!

INTRODUCTION

I believe you picked this book up because you want your life to change! You want to move to the next phase in your life. You want to be elevated from where you are, delivered from what you are in, and break free from what holds you back. Well, you can have all of that. It can be yours, and I will tell you and show you how.

This book was written just for you. And it is about your breakthrough. It's about breaking through anything that has got you bound. It may be that you feel you are at a point in your life where you feel stuck, complacent, or stagnant. You might feel like there's no way out, like you are in a rut and can't see the light at the end of the tunnel. Well, this book is about breaking through all of that no matter what the "that" happens to be in your life. It's about picking you up, turning you around, lifting your head, standing tall, digging your heals in, breaking through, moving forward, and looking upward.

The principles in this book will help you learn how to turn your finances around, get out of having to live check to check, or constantly worrying about how bills are going to get paid. This book is about being free from the same illness that has been attacking you for some time now. It's about how to propel yourself to the next level of your life. It's about seeking and finding fulfillment and purpose. It's about how to become more connected with God so that you can begin to hear directly from Him about His purpose for your life. This book will reveal a four-step approach that you can use as a tool to break through the strongholds in your life and position yourself for the awesome plans that God has for you.

I wrote this book during one of the most difficult times in my life. I wrote while in the midst of financial struggles, professional turmoil, and personal tragedy. And so I decided to write myself out of the rut that I was in. I wanted breakthrough in my life, and I sensed that so many others wanted it too, so I wrote—I write to help us break through. And the timing is just right, especially for today and the times that we are currently living in. This is said to be the worst economic times in the history of America right now. The recession has caused severe depression in the lives of God's children and that depression causes anxiety and insecurity and manifests itself into hopelessness and helplessness, which is not God's plan for your life!

You can overcome any obstacle. You can rise above any circumstance. You do not have to count yourself out of the race because you took another bruise to your heart and another blow to your spirit. You have the victory. Embrace the principles you will read about in the book—Believe, Give, Plan, and Stand. God will see you through to your breakthrough!

Gloom And Doom?
Not!

Over the last year or so, all that we have been hearing is how "horrible" the economy is, how "bad" it is going to get, and how we are in the beginning of the worst "recession" in the history of America. The news is discussed at your cubicle; they are discussing this at the water cooler. It is the primary topic at every board meeting. You can't even turn on the radio station because between songs or in between infomercials, you will hear something about the recession. When you turn on just about every television station, if it's not flashing on the screen, there's a caption at the end of the screen telling the world how many points the stock market dropped.

In hearing all of this, it dawned on me, what is all of this doing to our state of consciousness? What is it doing to our psyche, and more importantly, what is it doing to our spirit?

It is true, you know, that whatever it is we feed our minds builds a home in our spirit and our hearts that forces us to think different, rationalize differently, and behave differently. If we consistently hear how tired we look and drawn out we look or overwhelmed and stressed we are, well, some of us start believing it. Then we begin to feel tired, walk tired, talk tired, and act tired till it (the thought of being tired) sucks every bit of energy and life from our own body. But if we hear how good we look and how we look fit, sharp, etc, we start feeling that way too. There is a certain swagger in our step; we almost feel like we can take on the world.

The same holds true for what we continue to hear about the economy. If we are not careful and if we don't keep our minds stayed on God, we will become victims of the very thing I mentioned above. The negative, depressing news we hear daily about the state of the world, the stock market, the Fortune 500 companies that are going out of business, and the skyrocketing unemployment rate all begin to permeate our minds with hopelessness and helplessness. We start fearing that it could all happen to us, that our jobs are in jeopardy, that our mortgage company is getting ready to fall under, that our 401k is about to be totally wiped out. Then some of us go a little overboard; we run to the nearest BJ's or Costco's to spend $500 buying cases and cases of water, dozens of canned goods, and as much meat as we can possibly store in the freezer because we think the world is getting ready to come to an end, so we stock up on food. We know we are only a one- or two-person household, but yet something tells us that the world is getting ready to run out of butter, so we go out and buy pounds and pounds of it (sigh).

Okay, okay, so I may be exaggerating just a bit, but you get the point. The point is that we let the world dictate our financial state, our health, and our future instead of just trusting that God is leading the way in all of those areas. We may have in fact lost our jobs, we may have in fact lost lots of money in the stock market, and our pension plans may have in fact been jeopardized by the state of the economy, but the good news is that there is in fact good news! And it is that good news that I intend to share with you in this book.

I just want to share a quick story with you. I went over to one of my aunt's house one weekend. We sat down to chat a little bit, and I happened to inquire about one of my author aunts and what she was doing that day. The aunt that I was speaking to said that my other aunt went out with a friend of hers to go look for a new car.

"Hmmmp," my aunt said, "I don't know why she's doing that. No one is extending credit to anyone anymore, especially if you don't have stellar credit. Didn't you hear you can't buy a house, buy a car, or anything else? Banks are all going to be closing shortly."

I sat back and said, "What, what are you talking about? Of course, they are still extending credit."

"No," she said. "They are done. The country is running out of money. One hundred fifty thousand people lost jobs in September alone. It's going to be really bad. I don't know what I am going to do."

So I am thinking to myself because I dare not say it out loud (don't want to disrespect my aunt and all). But I'm thinking, What do you mean you don't know what you are going to do! You have a job, right? You have a roof over your head, right?

You have food in the fridge, right? You have a car, right? You have clothes on your back, right? You have your health, right? You have a God, right? Snap out of it! Okay, then I come back down to reality, and I realize that the entire conversation or rather the harsh blunt response I just gave to my aunt was actually just all in my head.

Okay, so back down to earth, I can only respond to my aunt by saying, "It's fine that she went looking for a new car. Sure she will get a new car. And yes, they are still extending credit to people." My aunt really had no response to that particular statement, although she paused (ever so briefly) and then went on to complain some more about how bad it is and that it must be true because it is what they have been reporting all over the news.

"Aiyayayahahy," I said. This is absolutely madness. What in the world are we doing to people's minds all over this world, with all of this excessive news of gloom and doom? It's almost like a slow and deliberate brainwash. I politely sighed and ever so gently changed the subject to more encouraging and lighter matters.

Later on that day, on my drive home, I thought to myself that what I just experienced with my aunt could very well be prevalent throughout my family, the city, the state, and the world. I thought about how even I have been feeling a little extra down myself. I am already experiencing my own financial struggles and not sure I can handle the additional heaviness with being surrounded by such depressing news all the time. It has certainly been hard to escape the reports about the economy and the recession, and I too have allowed my mind to wonder about what I would do if I got laid off or if, in fact, my mortgage company called in the mortgage because they were going bankrupt. Then I realized that I too needed to snap out of it, just like my aunt. So then I thought, What is it that we (God's children) could possibly do to help prevent other people from feeling insecure and hopeless through what may appear to be some of the most trying times ever?

Then I thought about my own financial struggles and the difficult time that I was having. And then it hit me. I was to write through my experiences. Talk through what I saw and heard people thinking and feeling during this tough time, including myself and my aunts. And as I do so, I can think through and subsequently share with others a plan that may help pull you, really us, out of this financial hopelessness and helplessness that we are feeling during these trying times. And not just with financial struggles, take it a step further to help with other life challenges that we are facing as well.

And it made perfect sense to me. After all, I too had been going through a really heavy storm in my life financially, professionally, and personally. And I recognized that it was not God's plan for my life to stay in that state but rather that I need to break through these walls and barriers holding me back and live the victorious life that God's Word says that I should and could live. Financially, I had been in a place of "just barely getting by" for some time now. And the recession hitting the economy just made matters worse.

As of right now, the moment in writing this literary work, I have $54 in my checking account, not too much more in my savings account, and approximately $600,000 worth of debt. I have no pension, and oh, by the way, I am thirty-five years old, single with no children. However, I have two dependents and two sub-dependents. How one can have sub dependents, and what is a sub dependent anyway? Well, that is a long story, one that will require a whole other book.

My monthly expenses exceed my monthly income. To put it bluntly, there is more money going out than coming in. And my expenses do not include those general cost of living expenses that a lot of average folk are able to do such as entertainment expenses, groceries, maintaining the house, gas or public transportation expenses, getting my hair or my nails done, going out to dinner every now and then, entertaining guests—you know, the day-to-day things that most people do even if they fall in the range of low-income households. But one of the things that I did make sure that it's included was my tithes (absolutely critical as that is the basis and foundation for any increase in my life—more on that later).

Given my current financial status that I just shared with you, I want to tell you that as I write, I am believing God for a complete breakthrough in my life. I expect to receive financial breakthrough in my life by the time I have completed and distributed this literary work. And not just financial breakthrough, I expect God to deliver me from the other areas of my life that feel like unending tribulations as well. I expect God to deliver me from my physical and professional storms as well.

With my finances, I intend to be completely debt-free. Now, there are two parts to my declaration. The first part is that I am believing that God will work through me and others to wipe away over $600,000 worth of my debt. The second part is that I am believing God to work miracles in the lives of my dependents as well. That means debt cancellation and supernatural financial increase in my family's lives too. Not only that, I expect healing throughout my body. I expect for the daily struggles and attacks at my job to end as well. It's huge I tell you—simply huge!—but not huge for our God.

Okay, so how in the world do I intend to do this? How do I intend to be debt-free in such a short period of time and release the professional and personal strongholds on my life and allow God to move in such a way for my "sub-dependents" to be provided for as well you ask? Well, let me tell you. I will believe! I will give! I will plan! And I will stand!

Just in that order is exactly the way that I have laid it out for you. I will believe. Then I will give. Next I will plan and then I will stand—easily said, not so easily done. Except that if you stick with me through the end of this book, you could also be able to do just that. No matter what the situation in your life, if you dare to follow these simple principles, you will open the door for God to move in an awesome way so that you can experience and walk in the breakthrough in every area of your life.

To bring about that change in your life that you are praying about and to bring about the change in my life that I have asked God for, you and I have to start by believing that our lives can actually change. You must believe that there is more out there for you. You have to believe that there is a God that has a plan for your life, and that plan does not include financial despair, perpetual sickness, emotional pain, hopelessness, and other challenges holding you down. But it must start with whether you believe—whether I believe. Therefore, the first principle we will explore to get us to our breakthrough is to believe!

First Believe
    Second Give
        Third Plan
            Fourth Stand

CHAPTER 1: Believe

If you can believe, all things are possible to him who believes.
—Mark 9:23

What Does It Mean To Believe?

What does it mean to believe? When we believe something, it means that we have decided to accept something as truth. We have credited it with veracity; we trust in the thing, concept, or person that we believe. If and when we believe, we rule out or exclude doubt. We are unwavering in whatever it is that we accept as truth. And so given that definition and the context of how we are to experience breakthrough in our lives, the next natural question is "What is it that we should believe?"

Well, before we answer that question, let's start with what we should not believe as truth. Do not believe that you will never get out of debt. Do not believe that you are in a no-win situation. Do not believe that you will always be sick. Do not believe that you will never get that job you have always wanted. Do not believe that you are destined for failure and you cannot succeed. Do not believe that all hope is lost. Do not believe that your life is the way it is and it will probably not change.

Instead believe that all things are possible! Believe that you actually can change and that your life can change for the better because there is, in fact, a God, and He does, in fact, have plans for your life. And no matter what it is that you need changed in your life, believe that God can do the unimaginable and the extraordinary. Believe that God's Word is true. And in His Word is your complete breakthrough. In His Word is healing, restoration, prosperity, peace, and joy. You have to have purpose in your spirit and in your mind that God can do all things. You have to believe.

Believe that if you obey and serve Him, He will give you the desires of your heart. You have to know deep down that no matter how tremendous you think the "ask" is, He is able to do all things. So go ahead and take the limits off of God. Do not include God in the category of man. Man may be bound by limitations, but our God is not. Equally as important, you must believe in yourself. Believe that God can, in fact, work through you to make this happen—to make anything happen—despite what limitations you may think you have. You have to be convinced that no matter how high the mountain looks, it can be conquered. Someone conquered Mount Everest, the highest mountaintop in the world. Someone even swam across the deepest seas. Didn't they need to believe in order to do that? You must and we must get enough courage to stretch our imaginations and think beyond what we see right in front of us. Think of it this way: There isn't one single thing that has happened in this world that at least one person hasn't been able to accomplish, conquer, or overcome—not one thing. And how awesome it is that it includes even conquering death. Death has been conquered! Jesus rose from the grave, and I'm here sharing this with you and encouraging you to believe because of it.

Now I don't want to be naive; I realize that as easy as I may have made all of that sound, our individual problems can feel insurmountable. Not knowing how you are going to make the next mortgage or rent payment feels like climbing Mount Everest. Keeping the lights on, keeping the heat on, or overcoming sickness or an addiction may feel like swimming the deepest seas, but just believe. Believe that His Word is true and that if He did this for someone else, He can certainly do it for you too. Not only can He do this for you, He actually wants to do it for you as well. He's just waiting on you to believe, to trust, and to ask Him.

I remember several years ago sitting in my apartment in Michigan, wondering not only how I was going to pay two months worth of rent but also how I was going to eat for the rest of the week. You see, I was twenty-eight years old then. I left my comfy job as a service delivery manager at AT&T to pursue my dreams of going to law school and becoming an entertainment attorney. And so I did. I saved up every bit of my money from the three years at AT&T, thinking I'd be able to pay for law school and keep a roof over my head while I was there. But somehow, by the end of the very first semester, I was already flat out broke. I was not cautious with my spending. I was careless and frivolous with the little money I did have. I had no residual money coming in from financial aid, no more money left in the savings account, and no line of credit extended to me. My mother had already retired and exhausted her entire pension on helping her four children get through the day-to-day financial struggles of life so that money pot was tapped out too.

And there I was. The rent needed to be paid, and I needed food to carry me through the week. At that point, I had spent close to 80 percent of every day going to classes and studying. The classes were three hours long, and I had two classes per day, sometimes three. And I was studying approximately twelve hours per day. There was really no room or time for a job in order for me to bring in any extra money. So what was I going to do? Well, I asked myself, What are you doing? How stupid could you be? You left a great job at AT&T, climbing the corporate ladder, but you gave it all up to do what? Move into a tiny apartment, go days without food, study for over twelve hours a day and beg, borrow, and steal to find money to pay the rent? (Well not steal, I was at least smart enough not to consider that. I mean, hello, I was in law school, you know.) And I sat with that thought for a day or so, but I was smart enough to know that staying in that stream of thought was not helping the situation at all. I realized that I shouldn't sit there wallowing over and over about what I should've or could've done differently. It was almost as if I started to believe that not only was there no way out of the situation, but I had begun believing that also I made the wrong decision in leaving my job to go to law school in the first place. I was entering a place of regret. I needed to snap out of it because it was either snapping out of it or staying in it, which meant eviction from the apartment and possibly withdrawing from school. That was not an option for me. So instead I chose to believe.

I believed that it would be all right. Although my natural eyes couldn't see it, I didn't have the money in my hands at the time nor did I have any prospects in front of me to generate income yet, and still I believed it would be all right because believing the worst-case scenario was just not an option for me. Giving up was not an option for me. So in my believing that it would be all right, I gathered up enough courage and decided to take at least the first reasonable step I could take. I decided to contact the rental office to let them know that I knew I was behind with the rent but that I would make the payment as soon as I could.

And so I did. I swallowed my pride (still not knowing where the money would come from), put on a stiff upper lip, pushed my fear aside, and called them to tell them I would pay the rent as soon as I could. The gentleman who answered the phone sounded as if he was about to give me the dreaded options—you know, "Pay this by this date or we will have to begin the eviction proceedings." He asked me for my name, and I told him. He asked me to repeat it again, and I did. Then he said, "Hey, are you Brandy Shiloh that goes to TMC Law

School?" and I said yes. He said, "My wife goes there. She's a first-term student. She absolutely loves you. She said that she was having a hard time with her Torts class and she went to one of your tutoring sessions, and now not only is she excelling in the class, it's actually her favorite course now. Wow, she talks about you all the time." Then he said, "You know what, Brandy, I'm not even going to put you in the system. Go ahead and make the payment whenever you can. I understand. I'll even change your payment date to give you a few more weeks' grace period."

My heart just jumped. I said, "Thank you, thank you, thank you." And after I hung up, I just thanked God. Even when you can't see where or how you will get out of a difficult situation, all you have to do is believe that you will, in fact, make your way out and you are half way there. Who knew that my blessing would come from the guy working in the rental office of my apartment complex whose wife happened to be one of the hundred students who took my tutoring class? The real question is what would have happened if I had not believed? And my not believing would have led me to not calling the rental office but instead sulking at home in a pity party, trying to figure out why this is happening to me and how am I going to pay my rent.

I am so thankful I chose to just believe that God would help to work things out for me. And it is so interesting because at that time, I was not spiritually mature enough to operate 100 percent according to my faith. I didn't really know how to use my faith the way that I know how to do now. I suspect that even if I did have enough faith to get me out of that situation, I would still have to actually believe that I had enough faith and believe that my faith in God would get me through. So I really just needed to believe anyway.

Belief In Action:
Confessing God's Word

Sometimes it's easier for us to just say we believe verses being able to say it and then actually demonstrating that belief. However, believing is so much more than just saying that we do. This may sound a bit repetitive, but it is so true. Believing is an action word. It requires an act or series of acts; it is a word of faith. And the Bible says that "faith without works is dead" (James 2:20). Believing requires a reconditioning of the mind, the spirit, and the body. It means that you are confident about something, and if you are confident about something, then you cannot doubt, fear, or hesitate. It implies that you must act on that confidence. It requires a step, a decision, and some movement on our part. Believe that the unbelievable is possible, that the unbelievable can happen, and that the Lord can deliver the unbelievable right to your doorstep.

In order for belief to be an action word, its actions must actually be demonstrated. And what I mean by that is if you are believing for some specific thing to happen in your life, there should be some step that you should take to act on that belief or prepare yourself for that thing to manifest or come true. If I believed that I would get out of the eviction situation that I was in, I needed to demonstrate that belief by taking action. The action or step that I took was to reach out to the landlord and let him know that I expected to pay the back rent and the current rent. I not only needed to let the apartment complex folks know that I believed that I would get enough money to pay them what I owed them, but I also needed to let them know that I would also have money to keep my rent current in the future. This is just one example of how to act on your belief.

Another way to demonstrate your belief is through the act of confessing. We will spend much more time on what it means to confess and how to confess as we explore the later chapters. However, very briefly, confessing what you believe means that you say out loud those things that you are believing for as though you already have them. In other words, we should speak those things that are not as though they were (Romans 4:17). These confessions are in alignment with God's word. For example, if you are suffering from an illness, instead of declaring that you are sick or repeating the doctor's diagnosis to everyone you see, you should say that you are healthy, healed, and whole. (Isiah 53:5)

If you are struggling from paycheck to paycheck and can't seem to pay your bills, don't keep talking about how broke you are to your friends, complaining about what you don't have. Instead say that all your needs are met according to

God's riches in glory. (Philippians 4:19) Our words really do have power. Let the words that come out of your mouth declare victory over your circumstances. If you believe that you will get out of financial debt and stop living paycheck to paycheck, then you should stop saying that you are in debt, stop saying that you are living paycheck to paycheck, and stop saying how broke you are. Instead, speak those things that are not as though they were. Say that you have all that you need—that you have plenty and lack nothing—and say that you are prosperous.

Now keep in mind, this is not just about saying positive things. Remember, saying the words without believing what you are saying is almost as bad as repeating how bad things are for you. It's not just about saying empty words, but it's also about saying the words with your mouth and believing with your heart and spirit that what you are saying is the truth. Back in those law school days, when I was trying to figure out how I was going to pay the rent and have food for the rest of the week, I not only had to say in my head, Lord I believe you will make a way, but I also had to say it, believe it in my heart, and then take action. I had to swallow my pride and my fear, pick up the phone, and call the landlord.

We should also be mindful not to say (confess) the negative that we hear around us. Like what I was sharing with you about my aunt, she repeated what she heard on the news. She confessed all right, but she confessed the negative about her situation versus the positive. The same holds true for you. Be mindful not to confess the gloom and doom news that you hear on television or from your family and friends who might be in similar or worse situations. Instead, say and confess your newly found belief—the belief you now have that says that your life can change; the new belief you now have that says that you will not always be unemployed or in debt or stuck in a failed marriage or suffer from this illness. Confess your new belief, which is what God says about your situation. And what God says is that you are a lender and not a borrower (Deuteronomy 15:6). God says that you are above and not beneath (Deuteronomy 28:13). God says that you are healthy healed and whole.

So if you are prepared to demonstrate your newfound belief by taking action and the action that you have decided to take is confession, then confess what God says about your situation. We will spend more time understanding confessing God's Word in the later chapters.

However, I do want to share with you that oftentimes, I think we look for God or someone else to act on our behalf. You know, like now that we believe and made at least one confession, we sit back and wait for someone else to take the next step; we expect the action to happen around us and outside of us but not through us, when simply it is just the opposite. It should be about us acting on the very thing that we believe and are confessing.

Belief In Action:
Reconditioning Your Mind To Believe The Truth

As I think about the example I used earlier with my aunt succumbing to the gloom and doom news about the economy, I say to myself as I say to them and you, don't just sit there listening to the glooming news day after day, watching the stock market crash and hearing your friends complain about the impending struggles that they predict are about to happen, but do something. Do something! Don't just sit there feeling sorry for yourself and replaying over and over in your mind how stressed you are. Why continue to think those thoughts? Why continue to surround yourself with the things that remind you of how heavy you are in your spirit? Let's not choose to believe the worst when there is another option, a better option. It is time to take your belief in action to another level. It's time to take steps to recondition your mind to believe the truth, not the facts as you see or hear it.

Believe that this state that you are in will not impact you forever. Then act on that belief. You must believe that the recession may fall around you but shall not impact you. You must believe that God has a concrete plan for your life and it does not include remaining in financial debt and living paycheck to paycheck. And then begin to start acting on that belief right away. Turn off the TV when they begin to report on the companies that are closing its doors after so many years in business. Turn off the TV when you hear them reporting on the foreclosure rates skyrocketing. Turn it off. When it becomes the entire conversation with co-workers at work, step away and out of the discussion. When your relatives call to complain and share their distress over the economy by whining and complaining, change the subject.

Then take another step to act on your belief by changing how you think about what is going on around you. Start replacing the gloom and doom news with good news, the truth. That's right. Replace the bad news with good news and not just any good news but the good news. Open the Bible and read the Word, put on your iPod, and listen to some uplifting Christian music. Replace the negative thoughts with thoughts of prosperity. Replace thoughts of sickness and disease with thoughts of wellness and healing. Replace thoughts of struggle and hardship with thoughts of victory and breakthrough. Recondition your mind!

I honestly believe that the key to deliverance from any of the things in our life that present themselves as challenges keeping us back, whether it is our finances, our jobs, or our social life—whatever it is—I believe the key to deliverance from all of those things is belief. You need only believe you will be delivered and you will, in fact, be delivered. Life's circumstances can be so hard and challenging to us mentally, physically, and spiritually. But they are only as challenging to us as we allow them to be. So don't allow the negative things you hear to permeate your mind and consume your thoughts. Decide to change that by hearing and watching what God says

Brandy D. Shiloh, Esq.

about your situation. Decide to recondition your mind through what you put into it. That means stepping away from the people, places, and things that only tell you how bad it is or remind you of how bad off you are. You don't have to hear it or see it. You can choose to hear and see something else. Go ahead and pull out God's Word. Read the Bible and attend a church service. Spend time reading, hearing, or watching something that reminds you of what you have been believing God for in the first place.

Although I have spent the last couple of pages focusing on belief being an action word, it really does bear repeating because it really is so critical for you to understand why it is that belief is an action word and why it actually requires us to make a move on our part. And once you do get it and fully understand its importance, then the question becomes, well, "What is the next move on our part that is required in order to exercise or operationalize our belief? What is the next action that we should take? Well, I think the answer to that question is it depends. It depends on what it is that you are believing God for? Remember, believing presupposes that you have made the decision to accept as truth a certain fact or circumstance; in this case, it really should be God's Word. And if you are doing that, then essentially, you should ignore or get rid of any thought or belief that is contrary to what you have decided to believe—what you have accepted as truth.

Okay, so now you are at a point where you accept one thing as truth and you have discarded or cast away anything to the contrary. Now that you have done that, you can go ahead and act on your belief. Start by preparing for the thing that you have accepted as truth. Prepare for it to come to fruition; prepare for it to become a reality in your life. Take the necessary steps to make that thing (the thing that you have accepted as truth) happen. So if you believe that your current state of being unemployed will end soon and that you will get a job, then begin to act on that belief through what you say next and what you do next. Begin to make arrangements for child care so that when you start work, the kids are cared for. Get your hair done or get a haircut in preparation for getting called in for your interview. Stand in expectation for the phone to ring with a job offer. Change your words. When folks ask you about your employment status, you say things like "It is going well. I begin my new job very soon." You have stopped saying you are broke, and you now say I have more than enough.

Belief In Action:
Casting Cares

The act of believing is also like the act of casting your cares. Because now that you have accepted something as truth and that something as truth is tied to the Word of God, it's almost as if you don't have to worry about it anymore. You can let it go now; you can release it. You have now cast your cares, that is, your worries, your concerns, and your troubles away. As the Word of God says, "Cast your cares on the Lord for His yoke is easy and His burden light" (Mathew 11:30). When you do that, you no longer have to worry about it anymore.

I was recently reminded of how deliberate the words in the Bible actually are. My very dear friend whom I call my "Iron" because she is my spiritual coach in times of weakness and serves to sharpen my spirit when I allow it to become dull (Proverbs 27:17), reminded me to reread that scripture (Mathew 11:30) and think about it carefully. This was important for me to hear at this time because I started doubting in my spirit and had almost begun to give up on believing that I would break through the strongholds that were holding me down. I had been feeling overwhelmed by the continual challenges I was facing at work. I had not been feeling well and had low energy for some time and was still going through pretty serious financial struggles as well. So she stepped in as she often did to help pull me back on track during my moment of weakness. Iron said that the Lord is very deliberate in using the word cast. She said, "Notice that the scripture doesn't just say sit still and God will pick up your cares, worries, and burdens and remove them from you. No, you have got to cast them."

So I decided to take a closer look at that scripture. The word cast as it is used in this particular scripture of the Bible is used as the verb in the sentence. And we know that a verb is an action word. The dictionary defines the word cast as something to throw, hurl, or fling. It goes on to say "to throw off or away," and as you read the definition or the different context in which the word is used, it even says "to cause to fall upon something or in a certain direction, to send forth." Wow, what a revelation it was for me. That means we can throw off our cares (our burdens, worries, troubles, etc.). We can actually get them off of us and give it to someone else. That someone else is not just anyone, but the Lord. Pick up the heaviness of confusion; pick up your stress and your doubt—pick it up. "From where?" you ask, pick it up off of your heart and your spirit. Lift it off of your shoulders. Be bold enough to stand up straight, grab it, lift it, and throw it off of you. Insecurities—take it off of you. Financial despair—take it off of you. Trouble in your marriage—get it off of you. Fear and regret—grab it off of your shoulders and hurl it.

"Cast your cares on me," says the Lord (1 Peter 5:7). Take those worries and stresses; remove them from your mind, and stop worrying about it. Don't allow it to consume your thoughts. Once you cast it, you become free from it. Free means you don't have to worry about it any longer. It is no longer your problem to solve. Go ahead and give it to the Lord. Cast your cares on Him because His burden is light and He cares for you.

So go ahead and do it. Believe the Word of God for your life and act on your belief. Believe that your life can and will change. Believe that you will overcome the temporary challenges you are facing. Believe that God wants better for you. Believe that God has better for you. And once you can begin to do that by acting on your belief through confessing and through reconditioning your mind and casting your cares, you must be mindful not to be distracted by destructive thinking.

Continue To Believe:
Don't Be Distracted By Destructive Thinking

As you know, I am actually believing God for deliverance from many things during the writing of this work—most recently, from persecution and financial debt. And what I have recognized is that if the devil can shake your belief even just a little bit, he can open the door to causing destruction in your life. Now, do not just think that destruction only applies to damaging physical things such as buildings being destroyed, natural disasters, or even physical harm. That is certainly one type of destruction. However, destruction can also mean so much more. Destruction can happen when we lose faith in the Lord or when we steer away from His plans for our lives. That particular type of destruction could lead to thoughts of fear and doubt, and it could lead to thoughts of hopelessness. We start to think that our situation will never get better. We start to believe that we will always live in this rut or be bound by this stronghold. That type of destruction is actually destructive to our spirit, to our confidence, and to our faith and belief. And for many, that type of destructive thinking leads us to a state of depression.

Just think about it for a moment. Isn't it destructive to be on a path of prosperity and then to be removed from that path? How about to be on a path of healing and then, all of sudden, start feeling sick again? Isn't it destructive to finally have identified God's plan and purpose for your life and then allow even a hint of doubt? And that little hint of doubt can simply start with the whispering in your ear that you can't do it—that nobody comes back from that sort of debt. And now that there is the introduction of these negative thoughts into your mind, you are thrown off course. You start thinking that you actually won't ever be able to overcome this personal storm. Essentially you start to believe the thoughts of doubt and the fear instead of believing God's Word. Your whole life is now being picked up from the course of victory and success to a path of fear and defeat, that is, destructive thinking.

That it is why it is so important to act on your belief by taking steps to prepare for the very thing that you are believing for to come to reality. It is why it is important to stay away from things that can be destructive to your belief. When you are busy believing and acting on your belief, you have little time to focus on those untruths in your life. That is also why it is so important to recondition your mind by stop listening to news of gloom and doom or the naysayers and replacing it with the Word of God. You must speak those things that are not as though they were by confessing with your mouth what God says you can have and are entitled to because He loves you and has plans for your life.

Belief In Action:
Avoiding Unbelief, Shaken Belief, Or Disbelief

The funny thing about exercising those principles of belief is that you really do have to make a conscious effort to exercise these principles consistently because you never know when you are going to need them. You never know when you will have to actually use what you have learned in real-life day-to-day situations. You don't know when the enemy of doubt or fear will try to shake your belief or pull you off of your path to breakthrough.

Just yesterday, I called a colleague of mine from work. She appeared to have someone in her office and could not talk. But I noticed that her voice was a little shaky, and it sounded as if she was crying. She kept saying that she needed to call me back and that she could not talk right now.

Earlier that day, I had been feeling a little heavy and a little down. I had wondered if the work that I was doing at my job was in fact what the Lord wanted me to do—wondered if, in fact, I should even stay at the job or go look for something else. You see, I had been having challenging times at my job. I had been personally attacked by the staff. And it was the most vicious and devastating attack I had ever experienced before in my life. As a matter of fact, it was the only attack I experienced in my life. And going through it was devastating enough that I wanted to just quit. I wanted to walk away. I wanted to resign so bad that I was willing to do so even knowing that I had family members that relied on my income. I felt that this job did not pay me enough to be the victim of this type of hatred. So I really wanted to leave and had pretty much made plans to do so.

But earlier in the month, during the time of the attacks at the job, God spoke to me. Now I have to honestly tell you that although I thought I had a pretty good relationship with God and I was going to church on the regular basis, I really had not been used to hearing God speak directly to me or even recognize the voice of God. After all, I was really in no position to hear from God because I was shaken in my belief and certainly had not developed my faith the way it is now.

I was so hurt by the turmoil at work and my financial struggles that I really had stopped believing in me. I did not read the Bible enough to even focus on what God's Word said about me. As a matter of fact, I almost started believing the horrible things that were said about me during the attack. I doubted myself; I questioned my own integrity and certainly questioned whether God actually had a plan for my life. I was unsure of my career, my personal ambition, and my relationship with God. Nevertheless, God spoke to me during my lowest point of that time. He told me to get up and shake it off. He said that He had work for me to do. And after He did that, I began to strengthen my belief in Him. I started to understand His will for my life, and I started to believe in myself again. And I had been doing quite well up until yesterday.

Somehow I allowed the enemy to introduce doubt and fear into my mind. All those thoughts about quitting, regret, and hopelessness had resurfaced for me. Sometimes when we are on shaky ground with our belief and faith, we become more susceptible to thinking worst-case scenarios for normal day-to-day situations. Where once we might have approached a situation or circumstance optimistically, believing it would be fine and that all things would work out, we now watch that thought process go right out the window. Our optimistic approach has changed. When you are in a state of shaken belief, almost everything that comes up—no matter how big or little it is—creates the fear and doubt in our minds. It is as if the things that cause doubt and fear into our spirit are all around us, trying to take us off course—trying to take our minds away from being focused on the truth of the Word of God. We start to expect the worst-case scenario for everything, including normal everyday life events. And that is what happened to me yesterday.

At the particular time when I called my colleague at the job, I had really been exhausted by all that had been happening at work. The trials at the job had been going on for weeks, and it felt like it was all just wearing me down. It was getting harder and harder for me to stand firm in my belief. When she answered the phone, I heard a different tone in her voice. It sounded as if she had been crying. I noticed that she was rushing me off the phone. So my mind went directly to wondering, What horrible thing has happened now? I assumed that she was crying because yet again something hurtful and painful had happened at the job. So from the time that she hung up until the time that she was able to call me back, all kind of destructive thoughts went through my mind. I thought that they had launched yet another hateful attack on me, or worse, they physically tried to attack her or others at the job and that things were spiraling out of control.

The fact that I was out of the office that day didn't help at all. As a matter of fact, it just made things worse. My mind went straight to worst-case scenarios. I thought maybe there was a threat on my life, or that they vandalized her car. I mean, my mind was on a path of destruction all because I opened the door to doubt and fear—all because I stopped believing just for that split second what the Lord had already spoken to me and had confirmed for me. Because I opened the door to doubt or rather disbelief, the enemy attempted to take advantage of it and interject thoughts of destruction and fear.

Well, fear is not of the Lord (2 Timothy 1:7). And if we operate according to our belief in God's Word, those things in our lives that cause us hurt or pain or fear don't quite have the same affect on us anymore. When we stand firm in our belief (believing God's Word and will for our lives), when we consistently confess our beliefs, and when we cast our cares enough to act on our belief, things begin to change for us during hard times. Our recovery time during tragedy or daily struggles is quicker; our healing time is shorter.

So it had to be only five minutes that I waited before my colleague called me back. But it felt like a lifetime since all of those destructive thoughts went through my head. And when she did finally call me back (sigh), she told me that there was absolutely nothing wrong. Nothing. I had been hearing things. There was no crying, no sighing, and no sniffling. She just had somebody in her office and could not speak at the time. As a matter of fact, she was actually happy. And the shakiness in her voice or the different tone that I detected was because she had been laughing with whomever was in her office. Amazing how easy it is at times to be thrown off track.

Simply not being steadfast in belief creates an opportunity for destructive thoughts to shake our confidence and our peace. It creates an opportunity for us to be in a state of shaken belief.

Most people feel confident that they know what belief is. They also may make an intentional distinction between belief and faith, almost suggesting that being in a state of unbelief is not as bad as not having faith or losing faith. Well, I've gotta tell ya what I have learned through life's experiences—those situations that I have experienced even during the writing of this book—and that is not believing and not being consistent in your belief may be as destructive in your life as losing faith. When we are in that state of unbelief, we open ourselves up to doubt, fear, insecurity, and defeat. It's just like the example of what I was feeling and thinking when I called my colleague at work. It is almost as if we get to a place where we question everything and act on nothing. This can end up being a very destructive time in our lives.

Unbelief is not a good place to be in if we are serious about changing our lives for the better. And when the trial comes, when we find ourselves in a tough situation and are running out of options that would help pull us out, being in this state of unbelief is the worst place to be. It's analogous to us being stuck in a ditch and not even able to consider the obvious options or opportunities to get us out of the ditch because we are questioning, doubting, and full of fear. When we are operating in the state of unbelief (which is not believing there is a way out or light at the end of the tunnel), we are not able to even have enough belief in us to see the obvious route of escape. We can't see the big Exit sign or Get Help Here sign that is right in front of us.

When we are in the ditch and struggling to get out, all we have to do is say to ourselves, Hmm, well, look it there. There's a shovel, a rope, and a ladder right here. I can dig my own way out of this ditch with the tools that are right here in front of me. I just need to believe that I can actually do it, not get distracted by thoughts contrary to that belief, and then act on my belief. When we are in that state of disbelief, we tend to be clouded by the insecurity, doubt, or even pity parties when we get into one of those "woe is me" states of mind. And because we are in the state of disbelief, the obvious solution no longer seems so obvious. The easy answers seem extremely complicated all of a sudden. So let's stay far away from it when it creeps into our lives. One way we are able to do that is to recognize it when it surfaces.

Defining Unbelief And Disbelief

Other than the doubt and the fear, what does it really mean to be in a state of unbelief or disbelief? I have heard it said that we could define unbelief in two ways. First, it is where you do not believe because there is a lack of knowledge to believe. This particular type of unbelief means that you do not have all of the facts or evidence to be able to draw your own conclusion. It is an unbelief where you just do not have enough information to be confident in the truth or existence of something. You cannot accept something as truth because you were not given enough information for you to process and come to your own conclusion and confirm i'ts truth.

For example, in the natural world, a scientist might not have believed that the Earth is round because there is simply not enough geographic and archeological evidence, facts, or data to prove that the world is round. Thus, the scientist lacks the knowledge to believe or lacks the scientific evidence to accept the asserted truth of the world being round. However, the scientist's opinion might change when presented with enough information that he himself can scientifically prove to be true.

Then when he proves it himself, he can now accept the truth of the assertion (either his or another scientist's) that the world is in fact round.

Similarly, when it comes to believing in the Word of God, you may not have enough knowledge about or experience with God's Word to believe it or accept it as truth. You may not have picked up the Bible and read it for yourself. You may not have gone to church and heard the pastor's messages about God's Word. And without doing so, you have difficulty understanding it, being comfortable with it; thus, you are unable to believe it or rather accept the Bible as truth. Thus, you disbelieve the Word of God because you don't know enough about it to believe it or accept it as truth. What happens to us if we are in this state of disbelief or unbelief is that it can prevent us from living victorious, purpose-filled and God-led lives.

So for example, many of you who are struggling in your finances during this time of recession may not know what God's Word says about your financial situation. If you have heard people say and declare that living check to check is not God's will for your life and you can have all your needs met, you might not believe it or accept it as truth. Actually, it might even sound absurd to you because it is contrary to what you see in your bank account or the bills that keep piling up. That may be because you have not read it for yourself; you have not picked up the Bible and read it. It could be that you may not have gone to Bible study or church where someone can explain the scriptures to you and show you how to apply it in your life. You may not know or understand what action you must take on your part to receive God's blessing of prosperity in your life. This type of unbelief is where you just don't have enough knowledge about God's Word to accept as truth God's will for you to be prosperous in your life.

But instead, you look at the stack of bills on the table or the insufficient fund fees hitting your bank account. Some of you are listening to the news about the recession or watching the stock market daily or reading the newspaper for the section that talks about the unemployment rate. So now this becomes the information or knowledge that you accept as truth. This becomes the information that you use to form your belief about your financial situation because it is what you see in your day-to-day life. It is right in front of you.

The Word of God tells you something completely different. It tells you that you are more than an overcomer and that you are an heir to the throne and entitled to God's heavenly riches. Read the Word to know that He will not give you more than you can bear, that He will raise up someone somewhere to use their power, influence, and ability to help you prosper. That is what you should believe. But in order to get there, you have to read the Word of God. You should spend time with and fellowship with other believers who exercise their faith for prosperity. Spend time in prayer so that you can hear directly from God about His plans for your life and watch the truth change the facts in your life.

Then there is a second kind of unbelief, and that is where you just aren't persuaded enough to believe. Now with this type of unbelief, you have the knowledge and the information to accept something as truth. However, that knowledge and information just haven't moved you enough for you to be "persuaded" or convinced enough to believe and then act on your belief. With this type of unbelief, you actually read the Bible, you have witnessed a close relative overcome the most difficult challenges because of their belief, and you may even fellowship with other believers in church and have seen the wonderful things God has done in their lives. However, because it hasn't happened directly to you or for you, you are still not convinced. You still are not persuaded, so essentially, you are really still in a state of unbelief. What you have witnessed with family and friends hasn't persuaded you enough to completely believe. Because you haven't experienced what you've heard them say they've experienced, you are not convinced, you are not "moved" enough to believe and act on your belief.

While I was growing (both in age and spiritually), I would continue to look for things that would "move" me. I was looking for some miraculous event that would just touch the inner part of me so much that I would be moved to act. What do I mean when I say "moved"? I guess, for me, it was that I needed to always feel inspired. It was like I could not, or rather would not, do anything unless I was inspired to. Imagine that. Imagine always having to wait for some motivation before you acted on something, whether it was the need to be inspired to do a favor for someone, needing to be inspired to go to church, and even needing to be inspired to hang out with friends. Either way, during those early years, if I was to do anything, I did it because I had to be "moved" or inspired to do it.

I was raised in the church. I heard what folks in the church said that God did for them. I have even seen Him work in my own family, but because it didn't happen to me and for me, I was not moved to believe and act on that belief. The bottom line was that I was always looking for some external force to get me to act—to encourage or inspire me to take some sort of action. I guess I was the unbeliever that was eager to believe but possibly not persuaded enough to act. Instead I waited for someone or something to persuade me. The mere fact that persuasion is needed suggests that you cannot do whatever it is that you need to do on your own. You are looking for or you require or you need some outside force or outside person to get you to the point that you think you need to get to in order to believe. It suggests that you are incapable of doing it on your own. Well, that is simply not true. It took me some time to figure this out for myself, but I realized that you do not need to look anywhere else other than what is already inside of you.

Christ lives inside of us—in each and every one of us. If we want to believe something or if we want to achieve something, we need only to look deep down inside of us for inspiration. The strength that we need, we already have. The courage we need to take the first step, we already have. The talent or gift we need to operate in accordance with what we believe God has directed us to do is already inside of us. The strength that we need to get out and stay out of debt is already in us. The courage we need to break any stronghold that is holding us back is already in us. We need only believe.

Believe In You

You have to believe in you. If you want your life to change, you must believe in yourself enough to allow your life to change. Believe that you can get out of debt. Believe that the illness will end and that you will recover. Believe that you will not be unemployed forever but that you have the necessary skills and the winning personality that would make any employer crazy not to hire you. Believe that your marriage will last and that your kids will grow to be successful God-fearing adults. Believe in you.

Once we get to a point where we believe God and believe His word, we become confident that, yes, God can provide, will provide, and wants to provide. We become confident in knowing that He can change our circumstances, but more often than not, we forget that He will use us to do it. He needs to work through us to change our lives and our circumstances. And we have to be convinced that He has placed everything we need already in us to make it happen. Yes, He will use you.

So believe in not only your heavenly Father, but believe in the faith that your heavenly Father has in you to accomplish it.

As I mentioned earlier, getting out of the financial rut that we are in may, in fact, feel like climbing Mount Everest. Overcoming struggles of addiction may feel like swimming the deepest sea. But know that any and everything we need to break those strongholds in our life, we already have. It is already available to us. We need to dig way down deep on the inside of us and pull it out. We are naturally courageous. We are naturally strong, and we are naturally wise. That's part of the reason why God gave us dominion over the earth (Genesis 1:26). He's already planted in us everything we need to dominate, to overcome, and to prevail.

God just doesn't want us getting by. He doesn't just want us breaking through the stronghold. He wants us to position ourselves in such a way that when the stronghold threatens to return, we know what to do, how to do it, and when to do it. He wants us to have a breakthrough! A breakthrough is not only having the strength to overcome life's challenges, but it's also knowing exactly what to do when trials return again. It's the difference between going from a defeated life to overcoming defeat in one's life and to living a victorious life. God not only wants you to get out of debt, but He also wants you to stay out of debt. He wants you to be wealthy, and then He wants you to position yourself to help others get out of debt, stay out of debt, and become wealthy so that they too can be a resource to others. And it begins with belief. It begins with believing your life can change and that you can change. It starts with believing God, believing God's Word, and believing in yourself.

No matter what it is that God has called you to do, whether it's going into business for yourself or starting a coaching program at your job or even writing a book, believe that you can do it. If you have never done any of those things before, just know that no matter what skills or talents are involved, if you do not already have them and God is asking you to do this, then He will give you the knowledge, skill, talent, or resources that you need to make it happen. Consider Moses, who God asked to lead thousands of people out of Egypt. In order to do this, Moses himself needed to believe. He needed to believe in God, he needed to believe what God was saying, and he needed to believe in himself. He needed to believe that he could overcome his speech impediment. He needed to have enough courage to go into a country that he actually fled from to confront the pharaoh who wanted to kill him and to be bold enough to get the Israelites who had been enslaved out of Egypt. Now that's a whole lot of believing for any one person. But because God asked Moses to do this and because Moses decided to believe, God equipped Moses with everything he needed to get it done. He gave him wisdom and the right words to say at the right time. He even gave him courage and a sense of boldness by which Moses could stand in front of thousands of people and speak boldly and confidently to carry out what the Lord asked him to do.

Consider, Noah and what God asked him to do in building the ark. God told Noah to build the boat when there was no rain in sight. Noah had to believe. Noah had to believe that it would actually rain and not just rain but rain so much that it would wipe out everything on the face of the earth except him, his family, and the animals God wanted saved. Noah also had to believe that he could actually do it. Now that is a whole lot to believe as well. After all, was Noah an engineer or brilliant architect that he knew how to design the world's largest boat? I mean, the design was one thing, but what about the fact that he actually had to build it with his own hands and that he actually could build the largest boat the world had ever seen? Now, did Noah have the decades of years of experience as a construction worker? No. But God equipped him with everything he needed in order to carry out the purpose or task that God asked for him to do. Noah also had to act. He probably had to confess. I envision him declaring to his family and all those in his village that this was the Word of God. So understand reader that if and when God asks you to act or do something that may seem far-fetched or outside of the scope of what you think your abilities are, your finances allow, and your talents and skills enable you to do, just know that if God is asking you to do it, you can in fact believe that He will equip you with the tools and resources you need to get it done.

So I ask you today, what are you waiting for? Are you an unbeliever? Is it knowledge that you are lacking? Or are you waiting to be persuaded? If the answer is yes (that you are an unbeliever) and you fall into either of these two categories, you may very well be blocking your own blessing and prohibiting your own breakthrough. And that is not a place that you want to be. If you are waiting for your miracle and if you have been waiting for your breakthrough day after day or year after year, a state of unbelief is not where you want to be. After God's Word has reached you, after you have had the opportunity to hear from God regarding his plans for your life or even once you have been introduced to the Gospel of Christ and are in a position to do better because you know better, a state of blocking your own blessing and prohibiting your own breakthrough is not where you want to be. Your blessings could be blocked, your prayers could be blocked, and you could be blocking your own breakthrough—the breaking down of your strongholds—by your unbelief.

So get off of the shaky ground of unbelief. If your issue is lack of knowledge and that is why you cannot believe God, then get up and seek knowledge. If your issue is that you are not persuaded enough to act on your belief in yourself and who God has made you, get up, dig down deep, encourage yourself, and persuade yourself into the blessings of God. Everything you need to encourage yourself, you have within you. Everything you need to obtain the knowledge that you are looking for is right at your fingertips. Make the time to find the time to invest in yourself. Encourage yourself. Encourage yourself. Pick up, get up, and act on your belief so that God's promises for your life can come to fruition. You or we are the only ones holding us back.

Believe. "If you can believe, all things are possible to him who believes" (Mark 9.23).

CHAPTER 2

GIVE

Give, and (gifts) will be given to you; good measure, pressed down, shaken together and running over, will they pour into the bosom. For with the measure you deal out, it will be measured back to you.

—Luke 6:38

B reaking through life's challenges and experiencing a breakthrough in your life requires you to give, give, and give. Now I realize that you are probably wondering what in the world does giving

have to do with being unemployed or trying to get over a sickness or even resolving serious marital issues. What does giving have to do with changing your life and overcoming the difficult times that you might be facing? And you are probably also wondering, How in the world can I give at a time of desperate need? You're probably saying to yourself, If I am in desperate need of money to pay my bills, how or why are you asking me to give money?" The answers to those questions are exactly what we will explore in the following chapters. I only ask that as we do so, you dig down deep and apply the principles of standing in the state of belief that you have just learned in the chapter on belief.

Let me start by telling you a story about what my mother did just last week. She was walking into the church building and shivered a bit to shake off the cold when she noticed a young lady walking in at the same time. Except what she noticed was that the young lady was wearing two wraps around her but no coat. It was probably around fifteen degrees this particular winter Sunday morning. My mother says, "Wow, it's cold out here, isn't it?" The lady said, "It sure is." My mother says, "We probably should be wearing warmer coats, huh?" The lady nodded in agreement and then says, "Well, I have a raincoat with a lining but nothing heavier. Just have not had the chance or the finances to get a coat at this point. But I am fine. God is good and will take care of me." So they smile at each other and walk into the church building to get ready for service.

The church service begins, and Mom is preparing herself to stand at the altar to embrace and pray for any of the visitors who have come up to the altar for prayer. After she prays and is seated back in her seat, she gives a precarious look and then smiled. Later that day, Mom told me that when she was at the altar, she heard the Lord say to her, "Give her your fur coat." She said that she shook it off a bit and tried to focus again on the service, as she wasn't quite sure she heard what she thought she heard. But she says that she heard it again. The Lord said again, "Give her your fur coat." So then very subtlety, she asks the Lord, "Huh, you're not telling me to give up my $5,000 fur coat are you?" (Just a quick side note on the fur coat, Mom purchased the fur coat many years ago prior to her retirement and prior to the financial challenges we had faced over the last several years.) Nevertheless, Mom says to the Lord, "Surely, you mean for me to scrounge up a couple of hundred dollars to get the lady a winter coat of her own. Besides this is January, and there are really only two more months of winter left." But then Mom says that she heard the Lord say it again for the third time when she got into the car to head on home from church. The Lord said, "Another is in need. Give her the fur coat." Then Mom, now realizing that she has already said no to the Lord twice, lifts her head and says, "Yes, Lord."

Okay, so let me interject here for a second. When my mother shared this with me, I had a very hard time accepting it. And yes, I will admit my not accepting it was for very selfish reasons. Here we were, my mother and myself, struggling in our finances. And although the coat no longer fit her and she had not worn it for many years, her current coat was also just a raincoat with a lining, and my winter coat was about six years old as well. So technically, we both needed a warm winter coat. Yet here we are with my mom telling me that the Lord is asking her to give her fur coat away. I thought to myself, If we had money to give away like that, we would go and get coats for ourselves or, better yet, let's sell my mom's fur coat on eBay for a couple thousand dollars and help pay that month's mortgage payment. I did realize that Mom had not been able to fit into her fur coat for some time now, but she had not given up on it and neither had I. Needless to say, I had a most challenging time believing that what she wanted to do was in fact what God asked her to do; therefore, I did not believe or accept it as truth. So I sort of hinted to my mother not to give up the only warm coat she had. I entered a state of disbelief and was trying to rub that off on my mom as well.

But sure enough, my mother ignored my hints and subtle comments and decided to "believe" that God did in fact want her to give the coat. She decided to believe the Word of God that says that 'if you give, it will be given back to you. A good measure, pressed down, and shaken together, shall men give unto your bosom' (Luke 6:38). And so she did it. She gave the lady her fur coat. Once Mom made up her mind to believe what God said and had decided to act on it (by putting the coat in her car), wouldn't you know it that on the same day, Mom actually ran into the lady again. So she walks over to her and said, "Sis, I am going to give you my fur coat." The lady, thinking that she could not have possibly heard what she thought she heard says, "Huh?" So Mom says, "I am going to give you my fur coat. It is sitting in the closet. I have not worn it for many years. It is almost fourteen degrees out here. I am going to give it to you. Will you receive?" The lady overwhelmed with joy says, "Sis, you don't understand. I just prayed to God for a fur coat. I just asked Him for a fur coat. And I realize that I don't even have a wool coat, but here I am asking for a fur coat. But God is able. God is willing. Thank

you, thank you, thank you. God bless you. God bless you."
She said weeping, "Yes, I receive it!"

That very next weekend, still not completely convinced that
my mom should have given up the coat, I decided to scrape up
what little extra money I could and take Mom to get a new
warm coat. Now I knew that there wasn't much in my
checking account nor in my savings account, but I said, Surely
I can squeeze out the remaining $100 on my credit card. It was
fifteen degrees outside, and I refused to let her just wear the
thin raincoat, especially after she had just given up her fur
coat. So off we went. A family friend of ours accompanied us
as we went from store to store trying to find cheap prices for
a warm winter coat.

We faced a little difficulty in our store hopping because
although we found the right size and the right style, we were
unable to find the right price. Or we would find the right price
but could not find the right size. As we headed to like the third
store or so, our friend and I declared that we were going to
walk out of the store with a coat. We believed that we would
find it; we confessed it, and we acted on that confession by
perusing every single part of the coat store looking for the coat
we believed we would walk out of there with that day. We
weren't taking no for an answer. And sure enough, not only
did we find a coat for the right style and the right size, but we
also found it for just the right price too. And if that wasn't
enough, we found several in the right style, price, and size

until we had four coats in the cart. "Thank you, Lord," I exclaimed.

Okay, so we narrowed it down to two coats. One I knew I could squeeze on my credit card, but two . . . two, I could definitely not do. So Mom said she would buy the second coat. Knowing my mother, I knew that the money she was going to use for the coat was probably grocery money, electricity bill money, or some bill money that she was getting ready to spend on a coat. But I let it go and decided not to fight her on this one. Okay, so we headed to the register and placed the coats on the counter. Mom turned around to go put the cart back, and I went and stood next to my grandmother to help her walk up to the counter. And in that matter of moments, our friend bought both coats.

I was completely astounded. I said, "Are you sure? Are you sure?"

"Yes," she said unequivocally.

"Amen," I said. "Amen!"

Mom comes back to the register and finds that our friend had bought both of her coats. She was overwhelmed with thanksgiving and joy. "Thank you, Father," she said. "Thank you, thank you, thank you."

As we headed back to the car, I said to Mom, "You gave up one coat and received two in return." "Amen," she said. "Amen."

Now, of course, I made it seem like that was a lesson for her, but in all actuality, it was really a lesson for me, especially since I was the one who was unwilling in my spirit to believe what God told her to do. I was the one who doubted and did not trust God's Word about giving. But I was so thankful that my mother decided not to listen to me but believed God and in the Word of God instead. The other lesson I learned here is that while a closed hand will not be able to give, it will not be able to receive either. Mom was obedient, and because she was obedient in giving, God caused her to receive almost immediately and twice what she gave.

Give Of The Very Thing That You Need

I shared that story with you because I want you to know that if ever you are in need—if ever you lack in any area of your life—give. Give of the very thing that you need. If you have a need in your finances, give of your finances. If you are in need of healing, look to pray for someone else's healing. If you need clients or customers to help support your business, support someone else's business. If you need talent, then lend the talent that you already have. Giving is the key to prosperity. It is the key to breaking strongholds in your life and overcoming what may seem impossible to overcome. So with regard to your question of how to get out of the financial debt, the answer is you can start by giving.

My mother needed a warm coat for the winter. The thin rain coat simply would not do anymore. So what did she do? She gave of the very thing that she needed. And in doing so, she received two winter coats in return. I like to think of it as the boomerang effect. When you throw a boomerang, no matter how much force you use or what direction you throw it in, it will always come back to you. Imagine that the very thing that you give is the boomerang. Now trust that the very thing that you gave, just like the boomerang, will always come back to you.

The act of giving the very thing that we need is an act of faith. It is the overt act or step that you take when you have decided to believe. Remember what you learned in the previous chapter: Believe God's Word and will for our life. And although we recognize that at this very moment, we are still struggling in our finances, yet we give the very thing that we need anyway. Our giving is the action or the step we need to take to demonstrate our conviction to believe.

The "Giving Plan"

Just last week, I said to myself that I was tired of seeing my account go into the negatives every other week and tired of spending hundreds of dollars in insufficient fund fees. I then looked up to the Lord, put my head in my hands, and said, "Lord, it would really be great if someone would just bless me with a huge check. I mean, wouldn't it be great if someone came to me and said, "You know, I just inherited a lot of money, and I know you are in need and I am going to bless you as I have been blessed." Then I paused and said, "Yeah, right, as if people have it in their heart to do those kinds of things."

Sometime later, as I pondered that thought, I said, "Well why not?" Why wouldn't folks have it in their heart to do those types of things? "If you have an abundance, why not give?" So then I began to imagine someone walking up to me and giving me a check for $500,000. Then I shook my head ever so softly to say, "Okay, snap out of it." But then I went back and asked the question again. I said to God, "Well, God, why wouldn't you do this for me? I have committed to do your will, to be faithful and obedient, to exercise faith, to tithe and give. Why is it so impossible to think that someone could come up to me and give me a huge check like that?" So then I heard the Lord say, "Well, what would you do with it if someone did walk up to you and gave you a check of $500,000?" More importantly, He said, "Who would you bless with it?" So then

I paused and said, "You know what, God is absolutely right. What would I do with it? Who would I bless with it? If I am blessed, then I should be a blessing. Isn't that what giving is all about?"

So I decided right then and there that I would go home and write out what I called the "giving plan." A giving plan is a plan that lists all of the folks that I would give to in the event I was blessed abundantly with money. And the interesting thing is that it felt like that was what the Lord wanted me to do all along. Actually, I think it is what He expects from all of us. He wants us to be good stewards of what He gives us. We should prepare a plan to give to others as it has been given to us. We should do this even before we think of all the things that we can do with the money and what we would buy ourselves. Think first of how you can be a blessing to others as you have been blessed.

I mean just think about it, reader, what do you think the world would be like if everyone gave? I mean, if everyone had the heart of a giver, how amazing the world would be. No one would want for anything. While you are preparing your giving plan to sow seeds of blessing and prosperity in someone else's life, someone has listed you on their giving plan and is thinking about sowing blessings and prosperity into your life. What a truly awesome place your household would be, your church would be, and your community would be if everyone operated in the spirit of giving. My guess is by the time your mind starts to worry about how you would get that bill paid or where you could get bus money for the week, someone would show up with exactly the amount that you needed to take care of all of those things.

Last week, in church, all I had was $29 in my checking account and $16 in my coat pocket. I intended on using it to get me through the next five days at work. I was to use the money for breakfast, juice, and lunch money. I knew I would not be paid until the following week, and at this point, I had been a pro at making a $20 bill last weeks. But while sitting in church and seeing that attendance had dropped, knowing that everyone had been going through tough times, I put my hand in my pocket and pulled out my little old $16, put it into an envelope, and gave it as an offering.

So there might be two things that you are thinking. One is why in the world would you give the little bitty money that you have left, knowing that you needed it to carry you through the week? And then, you are probably saying, "Why in the world would you possibly think that your little $16 would make a difference at all with the church expenses? The answer to those questions is that I simply believed it would make a difference. I believed it would have an impact on the church and on my life as well. Giving that money was an act of sacrifice for me—one that I needed to make to demonstrate my trust and belief in God's Word. It may not seem like much to many folks, but it represented a real sacrifice for me at that time.

The thing that we sometimes fail to understand is that it is not about equal giving; it's about equal sacrifice. For me, that day, it was a significant sacrifice to give $16. However, to someone who has $2,000 in the bank and needed it for a bill, it could be a significant sacrifice to give all $2,000. Either way, both of us would have given all that we had until the next paycheck, and both would be left with nothing until the next paycheck. Thus, we both would have sacrificed the same significant sacrifice, although we gave different amounts. The next thing to understand is that when God places something in your heart for you to do, for you to give, and for you to say, you must get to the point where you understand that you are being set up for a blessing. Clearly my mother understood this when she gave up her fur coat, although I didn't get it at the time.

God is looking for the believer. He is looking for the person that is convinced that His word is true, and He is looking for the person to act and follow through on that belief. I suspect that God actually gets excited when we obey His word, and I suspect He is equally excited when because of our belief, our gift, and our obedience, He can actually turn that sacrificial gift that we have given into a supernatural blessing. I realize that even after all that I have said, you might still think that the $16 I gave may be a tiny little drop in the bucket for any church and their expenses. However, the $16 amount does in fact matter when you are looking at the sacrifice. Besides, if there are 400 people that belong to that church and all the 400 people give consistently and faithfully at least that $16 per week, that would be $6,400 per week and $25,600 per month.

I bet you that a $16 gift doesn't look so bad now, huh? I think it is important for us to know that every little bit counts when we have backed our gift up with firm belief in the principle of sowing and reaping.

Going back to my conversation with the Lord and my newfound commitment to create a "giving plan," I decided to actually go through with it. I have decided to create my giving plan chart and share it with you, hoping to encourage you all as well. I started off by putting a plan together of what I would do if I were blessed with $1,000,000. But I didn't stop there. I put a plan together with a giving plan if I were blessed with $500,000, $250,000, $100,000, and so on. So I wrote it out and was serious enough to share it with you.

I will give it to	If I receive $1,000,000	If I receive $500,000	If I receive $250,000	If I receive $100,000	If I receive $25,000	If I receive $10,000
Tithes	$100,000	$50,000	$25,000	$10,000	$2,500	$1,000
Mom	$150,000	$50,000	$25,000	$12,500	$3,500	$3,000
Family	$100,000	$50,000	$25,000	$10,000	$3,000	$1,000
Church Building	$100,000	$50,000	$25,000	$12,250	$2,500	$1,250
Pastor and fam	$25,000	$12,500	$6,250	$3,125	$1,000	$500
Friends in need	$100,000	$50,000	$25,000	$12,500	$500	$500
Anyone in need	$75,000	$37,500	$18,750	$9,375	$500	$500
TOTAL	$650,000	$300,000	$150,000	$69,750	$13,500	$7,750

Now that you have seen and I have published my "giving plan," I need to be obedient to what I have committed to do with a financial gift. That means that now that I have laid it out and have committed to God, that this is actually what I would do with a monetary gift that He blessed me with. I need to act on it. One important thing to notice is if you look at my plan closely, you will see that I am giving away more than 55 percent of what I have been blessed with. The other thing to notice in my plan is that it does not even include any categories related to paying my own bills. There is nothing in my plan above that lays out how much money will be used toward canceling my own debt, yet I have committed to help cancel someone else's.

That is because I believe in my heart of hearts that it does not matter if there is not enough left over to cancel the debt in my own life. I know that if I operate according to the principles of the Word of God, I will get back all that I have given and then some hundredfold. I know that because my gift is like the boomerang, it will come back to me and all of my needs will be met, including debt cancellation. Because I operate this spiritual principle of sowing into the lives of others, in turn, others will use their power, influence, and ability to sow into my life and help me prosper. By giving, I set in operation the law of sowing and reaping. As I give, it shall be given to me in the same measure, pressed down, and shaken together. Thank you, Father. I believe and I expect it.

If you flip back to the earlier chapters, you may recall that I have asked and expected God to cancel all the debt in my life by the time that I complete and publish this writing. Well, my debt is approximately $600,000. And that happens to be the same amount that I would give away if God blessed me with $1,000,000 according to my giving plan. Operating by faith and not by sight, I understand that I am blessed to be a blessing, and as I give, it will indeed be given unto me in a good measure, pressed down, shaken together, in abundance, to the full, to the overflow, exceedingly and abundantly—all that I could ever hope or ask (Ephesians 3:20).

So why don't you give it a shot? Go ahead and do it. Get a pen out, grab a piece of paper, and write out your "giving plan." And as you write it out, declare that you are blessed to be a blessing, that you are a giver not a borrower, that you are a resource to those in need, and that as you give, you too will reap. Believe it, act on it, and stand by it.

Giving the Tithe

So what about the tithe? I do not think any of us will have complete victory in our lives without understanding the importance of tithing and subsequently operating under the tithing principle. Malachi 3:10 says, "Bring all the tithes into the storehouse, that there may be food in My house, and try Me now in this, . . . if I will not open for you the windows of heaven and pour out for you such blessing that there will not be room enough to receive it." If you look closely at Malachi 3:10, I think you will notice that God is not just merely suggesting or recommending that you tithe. This particular translation suggests that God is declaring that it is expected of us. The scripture says, "bring all the tithes into the storehouse." In other words, this you must do. And then He even goes further to say, okay, so if you are iffy about tithing and not quite sure if it is a principle that you should abide by or if you are hesitant or skeptical about what I am telling you to do, then try Me. Try Me out in this. See if what I am saying is hogwash. You don't have to go out and do a scientific, philosophic study on this. Just try me. Try it for yourself. And see if I don't pour out for you a blessing that will be more than you can handle. (Malachi 3:10)

We must understand the principle of the tithe. We need to know and believe that it is yet another way God is looking to prosper us—another way for Him to inject blessings in every area of our lives. But it is clear that it is up to us to take the first step.

If your sole objective is to cancel all debts in your life and live a financially prosperous life, you must give. I'll admit that it is probably easier said than done. However, remember that the first step in your breakthrough is to believe. There is a reason why the first step in this plan for your breakthrough is to believe and trust God. It is because of moments like these. Moments where I am asking you to do what may feel like doing the impossible. I am asking you to give when you are in critical need. I am asking you to give when you can't even pay your bills. I am asking you to give when you may be going through foreclosure right now. I am asking you to give even when you have no idea where it might come from. I am asking you to give when all you have is twenty bucks to your name.

Yes, I am asking you to give even some portion of that. To the layperson or to those young in their belief, this may sound utterly ridiculous. And I understand. I was there time and time and time again. I was there. But this is where you need to build your faith. Believe God. Believe what His word says about you. Belief is certainly an important step because not only am I suggesting that you give in order to get out of the financial rut that you are in, but I am also saying that the first type of giving that you should do is to give to God.

Now, because I was where some of you might be right now, I recognize that some of you may interpret what I said to mean that you must give to a pastor, preacher, or priest. And I can already see your eyebrows go up and your jaws clenching. But relax a second and hear me out. You have to see tithing as the biblical principle that it is. Do not see it from the eyes of church critics or pastor critics down the street in your neighborhood or those that are on TV talking about churches. These are the folks who are not shy about voicing their opinions about the so-called prosperity preachers of the world. You know, those critics who always talk about how churches are supposed to be for the people, but the pastor of the church is always driving a Cadillac, BMW, or Benz. Stop right there!

This is about you operating a spiritual principle in your life. It is about you believing God's Word and acting on that belief. It is about you and what God has told you to do. It is not about the church critics or the pastor critics. Unless pastor critics are going to pay your bills or let you move in when your house is in foreclosure and unless the church critics are going to get you out of debt and then stand in your place when it's time for you to receive blessings and increase, I suggest you make decisions on your own and not act on what you might hear folks murmuring or complaining about when it comes to giving. Besides God asked you to tithe, not the critics. Your giving is about you and God. Even though you might make the check out to the church, you are doing so as an act of obedience to the Word of God. And what the pastor or the church do with the money is on them. They are the ones that will need to answer to God, not you.

In the principle of tithing, God is telling us to give back to him 10 percent of what He has given us. When you are fighting to overcome life's challenges and trying to breakthrough these hurdles and trials, it is especially important to make sure that you do not get caught up in all the "drama" of people's personal opinions regarding their belief in God or His word. As I shared with you earlier, you have to be really careful not to allow thoughts of doubt or fear to interfere with your belief. Doing so only leads you to being in the state of unbelief, and you have already seen where that gets you. So be sure to focus on God.

At the risk of sounding redundant, we also need to keep in mind that God gives us what we have in the first place. And out of the 110 percent He has given us, He is merely asking for the 10 percent. But know that it was never ours in the first place. "All things come from You, and of your own we have given" (1 Chronicles 29:14). Sometimes believing and acting on the principle of tithing is challenging for us. At times it appears that we are more willing to put our faith in the lottery, Mega Millions, Powerball, the stock market, horses, or even slot machines at the casino than we are to invest in God's principle of tithing. Now understand that if you do those things, I am not condemning you. As a matter of fact, I have done them as well. I am not suggesting that you are a horrible person if you do, but what I am saying is that if we truly want breakthrough in our lives. If we truly want all that God says that He has for us, then we need to be serious and committed to abiding by this principle.

I have watched many of my friends and family go through it all. I have seen them play $20 worth of lottery tickets at a time and put hundreds of dollars in a slot machine. More times than not, they do not win. And the times when they do win, the winnings never last. That is because those things are meant to be short-term, nonguaranteed investments. But investing in God is the most fruitful, abounding, sure thing we could ever do.

So back to my point about why it was so important to begin this process of breaking financial and emotional strongholds in your life by believing. Because if you can just get that principle down, understanding and acting on the giving principle gets a little easier, and you will be well on your way of breaking through to your breakthrough.

Operating under the principle of tithing allows you to demonstrate your belief in this principle as the Word of God that it is. It encourages you to act on that belief and then align your thinking and words to confess the manifestation of what you are believing God to do in your life. Your belief will be so firm that no bill, loan officer, news commentators, or job can stop you from you getting God's best for you in every area of your life.

I Tithe But She Doesn't, How Come She Has Money?

As easy as I may have made all of that sound, tithing along with other principles around giving have not always been so easy for me to understand, let alone act on. Yet even while I am currently going through financial struggles in my own life, writing this particular section of the book makes things clearer for me. For some time, my approach to giving and tithing have been a little off the mark. I went about it the wrong way. I don't know if it was the many years in corporate America or if it was the training and education in law school embedding the analytical and deductive reasoning in my brain, but it appeared that I approached the Bible and my relationship with God in the same way as I approached work. I attempted to use analytical reasoning and attempted to apply logic to the principles of the Bible. It took me some time, but I realized and am still realizing that I cannot rationalize the Bible. I cannot rationalize miracles and wonders, and I certainly cannot rationalize Jesus' dying on the cross for me. There is no human logic to any of it, but I struggled to make sense of it nonetheless. I found myself comparing myself to people around me. I compared my situation and what I was believing God for to folks in the world that I knew that beyond a shadow of a doubt did not believe but seemed to be blessed anyway. These were people who were not tithing nor giving generously to help others. As a matter of fact, some of them seemed to be the most selfish people I had ever seen. Yet they had money as deep as the deep blue seas. To put it even more bluntly, some of them may not even have been law-abiding citizens, let alone believers.

How many stories have you read about folks that just fall into wealth or lie, cheat and steal to get money or other material things? Yet they don't have to worry about how the lights are going to stay on. They don't have to worry about whether or not the foreclosure notices are going to be in the mail. They seem to have all that they need and then some. Applying that to the principles that I had been reading about just did not seem to compute in my mind. It just didn't seem logical.

The second thing that I struggled with through all of this was that I would see one of my closest friends who made less money than me tithe only once in a while and didn't do a lot of benevolence giving to those in need (unless it was a family member in need of help). Yet she always seemed to have significantly more than I do. It seemed as if her piggy bank was never empty. Yet here I was, tithing, giving, and all, but somehow I was still struggling to pay bills. On several occasions, she would have to pay for me to have lunch at work or even help me by paying to get my car out of the parking lot. She often had to help put gas in my car even. I mean just two weeks ago, she had to give me gas money. I really could not figure this one out. I was certainly a tither and giver, yet here she is having to help me put gas in the car. Not only did she seemed to have no problems paying her bills, but she was also able to just go out and buy herself lots of extravagant gifts. I'm talking about $600 shoes, and $200 belts, and just last week, she just purchased a $4,500 Rolex watch. All this on the heels of her getting ready to buy a house as well. I'm like, huh? I don't get it. So then I say to myself and God, "Well, Lord, as much as she spends on all of these material items, she can't possibly be being a good steward over what you have given her like I have been a good steward over what you have given me. I save, I take care of my responsibilities, I tithe, and I give. How come she has more money than me? I tithe and give but she doesn't. How come she has money?"

Then it started to dawn on me. I am not my friend. I am not the folks I see on reality TV with lots of money. I am not that group of the "rich and famous." Their life is not my life. Yes I may want their money, but do I want everything else that might come with it? Do you want exactly what they have? When I took a step back and asked myself that question, my answer was no. So now I ask you, what is your answer to that question?"

When I gave it some thought, I realized that it is not about wanting what someone else has, especially if you don't even have a clue what they have or what it took to get it. For my close friend (and I love her dearly; she is a blessing in my life), I realized that we are different. I live a different life than she does. I have different responsibilities than she does. I have a different destiny than she does. And hear me, reader, different does not mean better. Different just means different. Different goals, objectives, aspirations, and calling. So unless we are willing to take on everything that we see in someone else's life, and I mean everything, we should probably just stick to the plans that God has for our lives. We should just stick to what He wants you to do—what He wants us to do—and then trust that we will receive all of the desires of our hearts in abundance and to the overflow (Psalm 37:4).

Make The Tithing Principle Work For You!

Let's make sure that you have the key elements of tithing down. So you already know that tithing is giving back to God 10 percent of what He has already given to you. So now that we know how much to tithe, the next key point of the tithing principle is where to tithe. The Bible says that we should bring our tithe into the storehouse. For that particular time in Biblical history, the storehouse was the place where one made their sacrificial offerings. It was the place where the people worshiped the Lord. So if we follow that same process, then our tithe should go to the place where we regularly worship God. Thus, if you are a member of a church, then you should pay your tithes at the church of which you are a member. If you do not have a church home or do not belong to a church, however, you find yourself frequently visiting one particular church, then that might be a good place to start.

I believe the Bible was clear about where to tithe for a reason. So tithing isn't just giving 10 percent of your increase to anyone and for any generic purpose. I believe it is about giving your tithe where you are hearing the Word of God and growing spiritually and where others are benefiting from the benevolence of the church—to a place where God can use resources to expand His kingdom. Your tithe should be given to bear the name and the work of God.

What if you don't go to church? If you do not belong to a church nor frequent churches as a visitor, I still think there are other avenues or places where a couple of the above referenced criteria can still be met. Look for a charitable organization that teaches the Word of God or look for a charitable organization that is benevolent to the poor, the hungry, the abused, and the neglected—a place where God can still help those in need, expand His kingdom, and where He can still be glorified.

I remember that in my college days, I was struggling with finding a church home. I was "forced" to frequent the family church on Sunday. As a child, I pretty much had no choice but to go to the church where my great-grandmother was a cofounder, my grandmother was married, my mother was on every church committee known to man, and where I was baptized. But I was not so thrilled about paying my tithes there once I became an adult. I wasn't too fond of the pastor, so I thought I can still be a good Christian and work the principal of tithing if I tithe to someone or some other charity. I decided that I didn't really need to give to a church. So what did I do instead? Well, I thought that I could just give money to friends, family, and any charity that I could think of or of which I felt "moved" enough to support. I figured that I was still being obedient to God by giving and donating my hard-earned money to others who may be in need.

I also did this by giving large tips to the gas attendant, the waiter, etc. And being young in my faith at that time, it made sense to me. I was giving to those in need, and besides, God knew my heart and He knew that I did this out of the goodness of my heart.

Hah, shame on me. Not only was I not obedient, but I also approached my giving almost like just another task. There was no thought behind it. And it certainly wasn't about God getting the glory because in my giving, there was not even a mention of God. It was about me being a good person. I didn't even say God bless you to the gas attendant who received that

$20 tip from me. And it certainly wasn't about giving the money to someone or the entity who would use it to help others in need, to expand the kingdom of God, or to share God's benevolence. For all I knew, the gas attendant could have used the money for another pack of cigarettes or a bottle of beer. I am not condemning the man if he did; I am just making the point that my giving was supposed to be in alignment with the principle of tithing, and I recognized that it was not.

Additionally, what I gave and how I gave could not even have been considered a tithe. I mean, I couldn't even tell you how much I gave, but I can tell you that I did not or rather had not calculated 10 percent of my increase. I was just giving. It was almost like blind giving. So really, I was not operating within the principles of tithing. Now it may have been considered benevolence, which too is important to God, but I do not think it is as important to God as tithing. God's instructive word regarding tithing is very specific in the Bible. We are told what to tithe, how to tithe, and even where to tithe. Back then, I hadn't quite grasped the full concept. I gave what I felt like giving and to whom I felt like giving just so that I could say that I was obedient to God. And in all honesty occasionally, it was something that I did just to say that I got it done.

The other thing that I found was that I was not giving on a consistent basis. I really did treat the act of giving as just another task. One of the things about tasks is that sometimes you do them and sometimes you don't. But either way, you can believe that if someone has called something a task, they typically are not completing that "task" with joy and excitement, which contradicts one of the other key points in working the principle of tithing, which is to give cheerfully. The Bible tells us to give cheerfully and not grudgingly (2 Corinthians 9:7).

So do not approach tithing the way that I did. Remember that the tithe is, in fact, separate from the gift and that it should represent 10 percent of your increase. Any offering that you give should be above the 10 percent represented by the tithe. It is not an analytical problem to be solved. It is a Biblical principle to be put into action. And as such, we should pay attention to how He has instructed us to give. After all, it is for us anyway. We benefit from this principle.

Giving A Love Offering—What Is That?

The offering is a gift above and beyond the tithe. It is also sometimes considered a "love gift" because it is given out of the goodness of your heart. An example of a love gift is a gift given to a charity organization that you know and trust will use the gift for those that are in need. And contrary to what I believed and was doing back in my earlier days of giving, the offering is, in fact, an example of what you give to family and friends who are struggling financially and could use a little help. Now, since I mentioned the whole family and friends thing, I want to make sure that I remind you that as you give, be sure to exercise wisdom in your giving.

One of the things that I found myself doing back in my "pretend tithing" days was that I found myself giving because people thought I had extra money since I was working in "Corporate America" and seemingly made lots of money. Therefore, what I ended up doing on occasion was giving money to show off or to perpetuate the thought that I actually did have lots of money. In doing so, my giving wasn't from my heart. My motive was wrong. I share that to say that as you give, be sure to search your heart and check your motive for giving and that you give from the heart.

It's possible that some of us (who are trying hard to live according to the Biblical principles of tithing and giving) are stumped as to why sometimes we have enough to pay bills, treat ourselves to something nice, and have money left over. But then there are other times when we can barely pay our bills. You might be wondering the same. Why is it that one day, there is a really great downpour of rain and another day, we are in the midst of a drought. Oftentimes when we experience that type of shift in our finances, it seems like a natural thing for us is to criticize the Bible or the church or the pastor or sometimes even God. We probably end up saying to ourselves that this financial obedience thing isn't really worth it. How can it be worth it if we still cannot keep our heads above water?

I have learned that this drought that we might be facing probably has less to do with God, the pastor, the church, or the Bible, but it has more to do with us. If our intent is just to have more money in our lives to pay bills and purchase material things, then we are going about it the wrong way. If our intent is only to get out of debt, then we are going about it the wrong way. If our intent is just to give so that we can say that we gave and completed the task of giving so that we can step back to receive our financial blessing, then we are going about it the wrong way. Our approach to giving and the reason that we give should come from our desire to please God and out of a compassionate heart to help others in need. So if many of you out there are trying desperately to figure out why you just can't get out of living check to check and just can't seem to get out of living in debt, maybe it's not about how much you are giving and to whom; maybe it's about what's in your heart at the time of the gift or at the time your tithe is given.

My "Giving Plan" Is Put To The Test!

As I shared with you earlier, I am strengthening my own belief while I write this to encourage you. As such, right this very second, I still struggle in my finances. However, I am committed to follow these same steps of breakthrough that I share with you. I believe, I will give, and I decided to go even further by confessing my faith and writing out my giving plan. In the previous sections, I encouraged you to create your giving plan as well. I also mentioned earlier that I would not be shy about sharing with you in this book the things that I have experienced and lived through while writing the book. Well! I have news to share! Right after I created my giving plan, God blessed me. He blessed me unexpectedly by giving me a pretty nice-sized IRS tax return check. I did not expect to get much money back, and I certainly did not expect this amount.

It was almost as if He wanted to test me. Like He wanted to see if I was actually committed to honoring my word to honor His Word with how I would spend the money—like He wanted to see if I indeed would tithe and give according to the "giving plan." Well, I took the challenge. I received over $10,000 but less than the next variable according to the plan of $25,000. So I gave accordingly:

— $1,600 to God (the tithe)
— $1,250 to the church building fund
— $3,000 to my mother
— $1,100 to family
— $1,050 to friends in need
— $500 to my pastor and family
— $650 to people in need (church, bus drivers, etc.)

I gave approximately $9,100 in tithing and benevolent giving to others. As I did, I was not only being obedient to the Lord by giving 10 percent of my increase in tithes, but I was also being obedient to the principle of sowing and reaping and giving offerings out of the love in my heart. All the while believing God to be true in His Word, standing in full and complete expectation that every single penny, every cent that I have tithed, sowed, given, and offered shall return to me hundredfold in ways of blessing and prosperity that I could not even have imagined. I believed and declared that every cent shall be returned to me hundredfold and returned to me not just in finances but in favor, in grace, in good health, and in breakthrough. Amen.

And even as God has surprised you with an unexpected blessing, you still get to stand in expectation for more and more and more until we experience the breakthrough that we have been believing God for. The IRS check was a complete blessing. It helped me quite a bit. However, I remain steadfast in my expectation for God to bless me continually with the other bills and needs that I have. At this very moment, I remain in need of refinancing my home. I started the refinance process some time ago but have yet to close the deal. The current interest rate on my home is higher than that of most homeowners. I look to save close to $2,000 a month simply by refinancing and receiving a lower interest rate. Because the mortgage payment is so high, I have gone as far as six months delinquent on payments. Yet and still and in accordance with my giving plan, I must remain obedient to God's Word and my commitment to stand firm in my belief. And it is because I stand firm; that is, I can give away approximately 55 percent of the IRS blessing that I received.

Throughout this entire process of believing God and living the Biblical principles of giving and tithing, I have been forced to learn that God is not on my time but rather I am on His time. So when I say that I am still waiting on Him to come through on the refinancing of my mortgage, I can do so because I realize that I am standing in expectation to reap because I have remained faithful in my tithing, faithful in my giving, and faithful in my trust and reliance on His Word. If I look at the facts in front of me, I could have said that there is no way that any bank would provide me with a loan with my current credit score the way that it was. My unbelieving eye could have seen that it would be silly of a bank to trust me with my current income-to-debt ratio, especially at a time where the economy is having the toughest times in recent history. They are picky with folks who have perfect credit, let alone someone with not so great credit.

That being said, I do recognize that it was nothing less than the favor of God that has gotten me to this point. I recognize that it was nothing but God's grace that has even allowed them to still be willing to consider refinancing my home as the economy continues to crash. Yet here I am—the bank still has my application for refinance, and although it has been many, many months without an answer from them, they have yet to tell me no. So I remain in expectation of God's blessing and favor over me for this situation because I have learned to be a giver and abide by the principles of tithing. I am in the final stretch, and I am not giving up.

Your Breakthrough Still Awaits—Keep Moving

So, dear reader, please understand that all that we have has been given to us by the mercy of God. And even if you did not have enough money to purchase this book, my guess is you are still blessed and there is an area in your life where you have been granted favor, mercy, and grace. If it is not in your salary, the blessing is in the fact you at least have a job, and if the blessing is not in your job because you are unemployed, then the blessing is in the fact that you have the skills, the knowledge, and the ability to go out and get a job. And if your blessing is not in your skills to get this particular job, then your blessing is in the fact that you have your health, that you are able to read this book, and that you are able to breathe—that God has shown you enough favor to continue to breathe breath into your lungs. Either way or rather however you look at it, the bottom line is it is all God's, and we should give cheerfully and generously when it comes to sharing our blessings with God's people.

So give cheerfully and graciously with thanksgiving. When you give your tithes, give them in obedience with the will of God and know that you are doing his work and that you are helping to expand his kingdom. When you pay your tithes, do it also with an expectation that God will supply all of your needs. And not just supply your needs but do it so that you always have all sufficiency in all things. Do it with an expectation that He will pour down on you a blessing that you might not even have room enough to receive (Malachi 3:10).

Let that be the framework for you as you move forward to the next step of the breakthrough action plan. I realize what it may look like to you right now, especially in the midst of this financial, professional, or personal storm, but hold steadfast to your confession of faith that God is able to make all grace abound toward you so that you will always have all sufficiency in all things, that you may have an abundance for every good work (2 Corinthians 9:8).

Believe, give, plan, and stand.

CHAPTER 3: PLAN

And the Lord answered me and said, Write the vision and engrave it so plainly upon tablets that everyone who passes may be able to read it easily and quickly as he hastens by.
—Habakkuk 2:2

You Are Almost There!

You are almost there! Your breakthrough is right around the corner. Now that you have made the commitment to believe in God, His Word, and yourself; now that you are beyond a

shaken belief and decided to act on your belief and confess God's best over your life; now that you have committed to giving your tithe and offerings with a compassionate heart, and now that you have created your giving plan and are standing in expectation for God to honor all that you have done, don't' stop now. You are right around the corner from your breakthrough. What you need to do next is plan. Plan for your breakthrough!

I recognize that it is at this step where many might want to give up. It is probably easy to think that once you have been faithful with the first two steps and have felt like your day-to-day struggles aren't so tough anymore, now you can stop there. You might think that by now you have actually felt the weight of the burden on your shoulders lift a bit. You feel yourself breaking through those things that were once stopping you from living a victorious life. You may have already received a financial blessing. Some of you who were out of work may have even gotten that call from that job you were waiting on.

For others of you who were bound by sickness and disease, you feel much healthier and stronger recently. Please, please, please don't' stop now. It is awesome that you have come this far. I know that God has blessed you and will continue to bless you because of it. But don't stop now. Your breakthrough is right around the corner. And it is not a one-time event; it is a change in lifestyle. It's being able to continually live the joy-filled, peace-filled, abundant-filled life that God desires for you to live. It's time to plan for it. Plan for your breakthrough.

A plan is defined as a detailed proposal for doing or achieving something. It is in the planning phase where we actually get to put a plan together to achieve what we said we were believing God for in the first principle of our process to breaking through to our breakthrough. It is the proposal that we put together to realize our objective for getting a job. It is the plan that we put together to realize our intent to keep our marriage together, get our kids back on track, etc. The plan represents our willingness and weakness plus God's will and supernatural power (Prayer of Jabez, Bruce Wilkinson).

I want you to imagine a bridge that spans 3,000 feet in length. A hundred feet from the water beneath it and the water under the bridge is ice cold and 1,000 feet deep. One side of the bridge represents strongholds, barriers, fear, and insecurity. That is where you are standing. The other side of the bridge represents freedom from all of those things, plus keys to a brand-new car, the deed to your new home, a job offer letter to any company of your choice, and a personal note from God written just to you and for you that says that He has plans for your life and He is committed to never leave your side no matter what you go through.

What lies on the road of the bridge between one side and the side that you want to get to is a set of obstacles. The road on the bridge is made up of three parts. The first 1,000 feet of the road is paved. The second 1,000 feet is made up very large boulders, and the last 1,000 feet is made up of very hot sand. Right after the hot sand is the other end of the bridge. On the side where you are standing are items to help you reach your destination. These items include a bicycle, climbing boots, a walking staff, sand shoes, a life vest, and a bottle of water. What is your plan to get to the other side of the bridge? Your breakthrough awaits.

If we know that good things await us on the opposite side of where we are standing, what is it that stops us from putting a plan together to achieve the good thing or to go after that good thing? As you read the above scenario, many of you have already mapped out how you were going to get to the other side. You already planned it in your mind. Some of you visual readers have visualized the entire 3,000-foot journey. For the planners among you, here's what you did: You took the shoe laces of the climbing boots and tied them together so that the shoes would remain together. You stuffed each of the sand shoes in one of the climbing boots. You put the life vest on, stuffed the bottle of water in your pocket or squeezed it between the handle bars. You grabbed the walking staff, jumped on the bicycle, and started your journey.

Your plan was to ride the bike until the end of the paved road section, get off, take off your current shoes and put on the climbing boots, stuff the sand shoes under your arm or in a pocket, and grab your walking staff to help maneuver around the boulders until you reached the sand. Once at the sand, you threw off the climbing boots and dropped your walking staff. You put your sand shoes on your feet, pulled out your bottle of water to cool you off from the hot sand, and then you finished your journey to the other end of the bridge. Oh, and for those of you who were above and beyond exceptional planners, you left the life vest on the entire time just in case you slipped and fell off of the bridge into the water.

What just happened here? You planned your journey to the other side of the bridge! You decided that what awaited you on the other side was worthy enough to believe in and important for you to have. You probably believed it would change your life. So you believed, took steps to act on that belief, and you planned your journey. Well, I have news for you. Your breakthrough is right ahead of you. It is on the other side of where you are in this point of your life right now. And you can have what awaits you on the other side because what awaits you on the other side is God's promises for your life: breakthrough, peace, victory, healing, and prosperity. What plan are you prepared to put in place to go after it?

Most People Don't Fall Into Success—They Plan For It!

Contrary to popular belief, most people do not fall into success. It doesn't just happen to them. Now surely, with God's grace and mercy, all things are possible, yet even God says that faith without works is dead (James 2:20). In other words, believing without taking steps gets you nowhere. God says, "I hear your dream Mr. or Mrs. Dreamer, but you need to take a few steps toward that dream so that I can meet you there to make it happen."

Take the time to plan for your success. Take the time to think through how you want the miracle of a debt-free, burden-free, worry-free life to unfold for you and even what it looks like. Get the visual in your mind.

When I was younger, I had this big dream of being the world's best entertainment attorney ever. It was all I ever talked about and all I ever thought about. Well there was something that sat between where I was in my career and my dream of being an entertainment attorney. It was something that I had to do if I were to see it come to pass in my life. I needed to put a plan together that would help me realize that dream. That plan included studying hard, getting good grades, taking the LSATs, scoring well on the LSATS, researching law schools, ordering the applications, and completing the applications. I realize that this example may seem just a bit trivial to you;

Brandy D. Shiloh, Esq.

however, it is important for you to understand what I am saying about a plan.

Whatever it is in your life that you are believing God for, it's great to believe Him for it. However, more is needed. Positioning yourself to obtain what you have believed God for actually requires you to think ahead, plan ahead, and effectuate the plan to make it happen. Although I have used my aspiration of becoming an attorney as an example, the importance of a plan isn't just about a career. What if you are believing God for healing from diabetes. Is it wise to believe God and confess your healing but not plan to change your eating habits? Suppose you just continue to take the medication prescribed by the doctor for your diabetes, yet you still have the same eating habits that include high starch intake and high sweets intake? It is almost like the medication from the doctor and your poor eating habits cancel each other out and the result of which is that you are no step closer to the healing breakthrough that you are believing God for.

What if you believe that God will cancel all the debts in your life? You recognize that you have more money going out than you do coming in. So you pray every night for a financial blessing, and every time you are blessed with extra cash, you get so excited about having money in your pocket that you go out and spend it frivolously. How can we expect deliverance from the financial burden if we continue to dig a deeper hole into the pit of debt? Where is the plan to realize the miracle you have asked for? If you have asked for a miracle of debt

101

cancellation in your life, here's an example of a couple of basic steps that you could take. Identify all of the debt you have and make a plan to pay them down one by one. Take a look at your income and plan to exercise financial wisdom in your spending. Determine what you can afford and what you cannot afford. Put your bills and their due dates on a calendar so that you are reminded to pay them regularly and on time. This will also help to avoid late charges. It may seem minimal, but these simple steps can go a long way to canceling debt in your life. Also, remember what you learned in earlier chapters: God needs to work through us to get things done for us and for others.

Planning means we need to work on walking in accordance with our faith, with what we believe. Take a second to stop and reflect on this for a moment. What is it that you are expecting God to do in your life? What is it that you were looking for as you picked up this book? Now ask yourself this question: What have you done recently to get at least one step closer to getting there?

It doesn't matter what challenges you are facing. Believe God's Word that the situation can change, and develop a plan that allows your words and action to align with the manifestation of God's Word for that plan. Then take a step to put the plan into action. If you are in an abusive marriage and you sought direction from the Word of God on your marriage, make a plan to get help or make a plan to get out (whichever it is you believe God told you to do). If you are living a life of fear and regret, make the plan to forgive yourself from things in your past and make the plan for peace and success in your future. If you are asking God for help in changing the behavior of your children, make a plan to seek God for his wisdom, stay steadfast in prayer, and take the necessary steps that allow for your children to change. Whatever it is that you are believing God for, there is a plan to make it happen.

There are some of us who do not think we have it in us to make it happen—to realize the thing that we are aspiring to achieve. Why most of us fall short is that we have a tendency to look outside of ourselves and find someone else or something else to do the work for us. We think that our job ends with believing and praying, and now that we said that we believed, gave, and prayed, we can sit back and watch it all unfold in our lives because we don't have what it takes to make it happen. But that is simply not true. As we learned earlier, all that we need is already inside of us. You just need to know where to start.

Starting To Plan

So you say, "Okay, I get it. I need to make a plan. Where do I start?" That is a very good question. One of the best places to start is asking yourself what it is that you are believing God for specifically. Specifically, not at a high level, but what do you need or want God to do for you specifically? What storm are you looking to overcome? What significant problem or life challenge are you looking to solve. And if there is no storm or life challenge but you are believing God just for a breakthrough to live a peaceful and joyful life, then what is it specifically that you need God to do for you? Start with identifying the "what" part of that question. And if you are really not quite sure what it is, just reflect back to your prayers. What is the constant prayer that continues to just resurface in your daily time with God? It may not even be about you; it may be about someone in your family. But either way, your prayer list is a good place to start if you haven't quite figured out what you are believing God for or what it is that you need for Him to do for you.

Once you have identified the "what" part of the question, the next thing that you should do is envision what it looks like when you finally get it.

What does your breakthrough actually look like? This part takes a bit of imagination, but it is a critical piece, as it will help to create a very specific plan for making it happen. So think about it. What does the breakthrough in your life really look like? See yourself walking in it completely. Get the actual picture in your mind. See it clearly, visualize it vividly, and imagine it distinctively.

I asked myself that same question as well. I am looking for complete and total debt cancellation in my life. And what does that look like for me? It looks like a breath of fresh air. It feels like me exhaling constantly and consistently, not just to catch my breath as I hold tighter, bracing myself for the whirlwind that is day-to-day life. No, for me, it looks like peace of mind, being in that wonderful exhale state nonstop. It looks like security and dependability—unmovable and unshakable. It looks like five different bank accounts: one for checking and four for savings. The checking has more than enough, so much more that it gets harder and harder to see the balance decreasing because the more I give, the more I receive, and I can rarely see the withdrawals because for every withdrawal, there is five times the number of deposits.

I see that I have everything that I could ever want and everything that I could ask for before I can even get a chance to think about it, because I would already have it. It is the overwhelming unspeakable joy that I would get from using my prosperity as a tool to bless people and win the lost. For me, it is giving, giving, giving, and even more giving. It's the joy on people's face when they are the recipient of a supernatural blessing in the form of a random act of kindness. It is watching the gleam in the eyes of someone who knew that they were desperately in the need of a financial blessing in order to stop eviction proceedings, when all of a sudden, they are the beneficiary of a random act of kindness whose dollar amount meets the specific need that they are looking for with having plenty left over to spare. For me, I see everyone around me, all my family, all of my friends, all of my family's friends—all of them—with every need in their life met. I see them not wanting for anything and even them turning around solely to be a blessing to others the way that they have been blessed. I see this book selling millions, being on the top bestseller list, never going out of print, and continually being a blessing to millions of people all over the world. It is seeing lives changed by reading this book. It's hearing you, the reader, say that you have experienced supernatural breakthrough in your life because you picked up this book and decided to reconnect yourself to God. For me, it's being invited to talk about the experience of my breakthrough on the Joyce Meyer's show or the Oprah Winfrey show. (Love Joyce and love Oprah!) And that's what breakthrough looks like for me. And it's a beautiful thing.

So think about it, imagine it, and visualize it. Get a crystal-clear picture in your mind of what it looks like for you. And write it down. Don't be shy. Put pen to paper as you visualize the breakthrough. If you have a picture of it, post the picture everywhere; surround yourself with images of where you want to be when you experience your breakthrough.

Plan And Write The Vision And Make It Plain

Okay, the next thing that you need to do is to get prepared to document the plan. Make sure that you pick up a journal, a notebook, a daily planner, or some other item so that you can script and outline the plan for your breakthrough. And as you do that, now think about whether or not there are any prerequisites that absolutely have to happen before this aspiration, dream, or goal can come to fruition. Definitely get those down on paper.

Because I am believing God for debt cancellation in my life, my plan includes writing down all of my debts and the debtors. As I list all of the vendors to which I owe money, I not only include the monthly payments but also the amount that it would take to clear the debt in its entirety. Documenting and writing down your plan is imperative because God needs to know in detail what it is you are asking Him to do for you. So lay this out in your plan as detailed and clear as possible. Spell it out not just for God but for you as well. Most of us who are overwhelmed with debt don't really have an idea of how much we really owe and to whom we owe the money.

It is so easy to lose sight of how much we owe because going into debt is so easy and such a normal way of life that naturally it is easy for us to not have a handle on it. So for those of you who are believing God for debt cancellation in your life, this may be the first time that you actually write out everything you owe, who you owe it to, how much you owe, and how much you pay on a monthly basis. You should also take this opportunity to write down any of the other areas where you spend money on a weekly or monthly basis. This would include how much you spend commuting to and from work and how much you spend on eating out and leisure spending—you know, picking up things every now and then like CDs, DVDs, new jeans, and new sneakers; money spent on hanging out; going to the movies; etc.

Oh, my speaking of eating out . . . well, let me tell you what I found while I was outlining my plan for debt cancellation. I had no idea just how much money I was spending on eating out daily, weekly, and monthly. I found that I was spending close to $350 per month on eating out every month. No wonder why I was having a hard time keeping my finances straight and being able to pay my bills. I was throwing money out the window and had no idea that I was doing it until I decided to write out my debt cancellation plan.

Three hundred fifty dollars is a lot of money to spend on eating out monthly. I mean it is a car payment for goodness' sake. Wow, $350 a month is $4,200 per year. If I discontinue this particular spending habit and start bringing lunch to work, I could save close to $21,000 over the next five years. I don't know how much more I can emphasize the importance of thinking things through enough to write it down in some form of plan. But please, please give it a shot.

The eating thing is just another example and reason why writing a plan helps you to get to the place you are believing God to be because when you write out a plan, you have the opportunity to start thinking about things and items that you would otherwise not have thought of or considered had you not taken the time to think carefully through the intricate details. It creates an opportunity to look carefully at your current state and the state or place where you want to be. Okay, so write out your plan.

Once you have written it out, you should look at what you documented and see if there is anything that you can do right here and now that will help you get just one more step closer to the place where you want to be. When it came to my plan, I had to take a real close look at all of my expenses and the money that leaves my account on a daily basis.

Then I needed to identify what I could do to help God help me to get to the point of complete debt cancellation in my life. Beginning with bringing my lunch to work is a great start. The same money that I save from not eating out so often is the money that I could use to pay down my debt. I also decided to stop using my credit cards as much. And certainly I stopped using my credit card to pay for food. Buying a meal, eating the meal, and paying interest on the meal before it has even had a chance to digest is pretty bad. So for me, it made practical sense to discontinue using my credit cards unless it is an emergency.

Please understand that what I have shared with you about my plan for debt cancellation is not just about managing finances. It is about realizing that there may be strongholds in your life that need to be broken. It's about recognizing that God desires us to experience breakthroughs in our lives so that we can live the life that He desires for us to live and promises. It's about taking the steps to believe that, give for it, and put a plan in place to make it happen.

You Are Closer Than You Think

Well, great job of getting this far. There is good news for you—good news for us. That good news is we are closer than we think! Our breakthrough is imminent. We can see clearly now, and it is a wonderful thing. Creating the detailed plan has allowed for us to see the road ahead of us and identify the few hurdles in the way, and given us enough time to move around them as we head toward the other side of the bridge. We are following the yellow brick road. As we move closer to experiencing our breakthrough, I want to prepare you for what might lie ahead. We already know that the enemy does not want to see us set free. Since we know that, it should not come as a surprise to you to hear that there may be times when he wants to take one last shot at us because he knows our breakthrough is right around the corner.

Do not be moved! But be encouraged. We need only stand and we shall be victorious!

CHAPTER 4: STAND

Blessed (happy, to be envied) is the man who is patient under trial and stands up under temptation, for when he has stood the test and been approved, he will receive the (victor's) crown of life which God has promised to those who love Him.
—James 1:12

Right before you receive the breakthrough; right before you get your reward from believing, giving, and planning, plus all the other things that you have been enduring over the many, days, weeks,

months, and years; right before you receive what God has promised you for obeying and serving Him; and before the walls come down, the barriers fall, and the strongholds are broken, you may have to be tempted and tested yet again.

And this test may be much different than what you ever experienced in your life. This particular trial might feel harder, deeper, and last longer. It may feel more painful than any other you have ever experienced. Nevertheless, just know that it is a sign. It is confirmation that you are on the right track. And because you have successfully strengthened your relationship with God and thus strengthened your inner self by believing in yourself, you can be confident in this very thing: God is with you, Christ is in you, Angels surround you, and the devil is defeated. Victory is yours, and your breakthrough is imminent. To God be the glory. Your breakthrough is here. Stand, stand, stand.

No matter what, now that you have come this far, do not turn around. Trials may come, but do not be moved. Have a conviction in your spirit that you shall not be moved. Take a step back to think about it, and look at how far you have come. Recognize the great strides you have already made in your life. You wanted your life to change, and it already has. You have already overcome many hurdles, so don't be moved by this one. Stay steadfast in your belief. This attempt by the enemy may feel a little different for you. It might not feel like just the day-to-day struggles and challenges that you face or just the normal stresses of life. This one might, in fact, feel like simultaneous deliberate attacks on every area of your life all at one time (professionally, physically, emotionally, and/or financially).

You need to know that this next attempt to pull you off the path of breakthrough and shake your belief is probably very deliberate. But it is deliberate for only one reason, because wonderful things await you. Success awaits you, debt relief awaits, happiness in your job and in your home awaits, and discovering God's purpose for your life awaits you. So if, in fact, you are tempted, tested, and attacked during this particular point in your life, it's because your breakthrough is around the corner, so you have got to hold your ground and stand!

Stumbled But Haven't Fallen

Within the last few months of writing this book, I have gone through but persevered out of the second most difficult trial I have ever experienced in my life. The attack on me was at my workplace. I briefly mentioned it to you when we discussed belief. With this particular attack, I experienced something that I have never experienced before. Next to the unexpected loss of my older brother, this attack and going through it was the hardest thing I had ever had to go through. Folks at the job decided to launch an attack on me and then subsequently created an opportunity where thousands of employees could attack each other, using a public forum to do it.

The forum was a blog Web site where folks spread lies and hurtful things about people, but mostly focusing on me. The content of the site contained horrible, painful, defamatory untruths about me, and I was devastated. I had never been attacked before nor fathomed anyone would have so much hate in their heart toward me to even do this. The picture painted about me was one where I didn't even recognize who they were talking about. It was an all-out attack on my character, my morals, my professional work ethics, my faith, and my integrity.

Some folks might not think that such a thing is a big deal. Not so for me. You see, one of the strongholds in my life was being insecure about what people thought of me. I had been a people pleaser for some time. I always wanted folks to like me. Based upon my own insecurities from childhood to adulthood, I tried my best to make sure that people were not saying anything bad about me. Instead, I overcompensated for my insecurities by becoming a people pleaser.

And here it was—all that I feared as a child and as an adult. People were talking about me. And it was not just small water cooler talk; it was a public forum on the Internet. The attack didn't end there. While creating this forum to attack me, folks used the same forum to attack others at the company as well.

And that is exactly what happened. They began to attack each other, saying hateful things. The horrible things said on the site included hurtful things like who has what drug addiction, sexual encounters, and who slept their way to the top; sexual preferences; disparaging comments about weight and physical appearance; information about where people live; who had ever been incarcerated—all kinds of things. The site became a web of hate and viciousness.

And where and how am I during this ordeal? I felt responsible—I felt completely responsible, hurt, wounded, in pain, and devastated. I felt like all of these people are in pain because I took the job, because I didn't help people the way I should have, and because I didn't do enough to get them to like me, and now what started out as an attack against me has spawned to an attack on everyone. I literally felt sick to my stomach. I had no appetite. I was not sleeping. I literally struggled just to make it into work each day. And God . . . well, the only thing I could muster up to say to God while I was going through this ordeal was "Why?"

At some point during my grieving, the Lord told me to get up. He told me to stop sulking and shake it off already. He told me to strengthen the spirit man within me and listen out for what He needs me to do. He said, "Get up, do you hear that people are in pain? My people are hurting!" And I immediately responded to Him saying, "Well, I'm hurt too, Lord. I'm in pain too. What about me?"

Nevertheless, I tried to do just what He said. I tried to get up. And it took some time. I started by just feeding my spirit nothing but the Word. In other words, I only read the Word of God and listened to the Word of God, and if I watched anything on TV, it had to be related to the Word of God and nothing else. I went on a Word fast—no music unless it was Christian music; no TV unless it was the Word. Then I began to start fasting and praying. God also gave me an "Iron"— someone who I could pray with, fast with, and work with me to help me up and out of what I was under.

As I began to be strengthened and encouraged by spending so much time in the word of God, I was able to "get up." And when I did, it felt just like the Saul-to-Paul transformation. It was like scales began to fall off of my eyes, and I began to see things with a completely different lens. I was now able to see that the people who caused me and others this pain actually did so out of pain. It became painfully clear to me that hurting people hurt people. I realized that the folks who began and perpetuated the attack on others were actually in pain themselves. I finally understood that what God wanted me to do was to be available for Him (to work through me), to heal the hurt of those who were in pain, which included not only those who were the recipient of the pain like myself, but included those who caused it as well.

Sigh. He allowed me to see the stronghold that had been in and on that company for years. He allowed me to see the hurt and the pain that these folks had experienced and have been carrying day to day. And it was at this point that He told me that the very reason I was there—the very reason He gave me this job—was to be a vehicle for Him to heal the wounds of these people while healing my own wounds as well. God was setting me up for a breakthrough, and I didn't even know it (sigh and exhale).

He wanted me free from the stronghold of insecurity and people pleasing. He wanted my heart opened long enough for Him to reveal to me (and for me to actually hear it) His purpose and plan for my life. It was to be a breakthrough of revelation—of opening my eyes, feeling things like I have never felt before, and seeing things that I would not otherwise have seen without experiencing this attack. Positioning myself to use this as a testimony to share, encourage, and heal others. Yes, it was a breakthrough of revelations.

Nonetheless, I might not have been able to experience the breakthrough nor have known that it was around the corner had I not been able to stand through it all. It took me a minute to be able to gather my strength and get up. It took me a minute to stop the tears, the sulking, and the wallowing in my pain and the pain I felt for others. But I did. And as God gave me the strength to get up, He also gave me the strength to stand. He encouraged me and empowered me to use the principles that I have shared with you in this book to be able to stand in the midst of it all.

God told me to believe. I needed to believe in Him and believe in myself. He put people in my path like my Iron that reminded me that He wanted more for me and better for me than lying around in despair and hopelessness. He used my Iron and my mother to constantly remind me that He has plans just for me. He told me don't quit and don't give up.

It was through this particular storm in my life that God gave me the principles of believe, give, plan, and stand. This trial at my job was not the only thing I had going on in my life. Yes, I was experiencing serious financial challenges. Yes, I was experiencing physical health issues as well. It felt as though I was in a war and the enemy had me surrounded on all sides.

The attack at work felt like being completely surrounded and now someone had just thrown a grenade in the hole, like the enemy was looking for complete destruction. But God used my willingness and weakness, along with His supernatural power, to get me up and out of the hole right in the nick of time. And as I was pulled from the hole, this is the prayer I prayed:

Thank You, Father, for revelations. Thank You, for a praying mother. Thank You, Father, that Your Word is true, that You are not a man and shall not lie. Thank You, Father, that you will never leave me nor forsake me. Thank You, Father, that my steps are already ordered by You. Thank You, that you have made my name great and no man can change it. Thank You, Father, that you have a plan for my life, that there is an anointing over my life, that this joy that I have, those folks did not give it to me, and those folks could not take it away.

In Jesus' name. Amen!

Your temptation or test right before your breakthrough may not be as painful or devastating to deal with as mine. Or it is possible that it could be even worse. The "what" part of the attack doesn't matter. The type of storm we are facing isn't as important as we think it is. It's what we do when we are in the middle of the storm that matters.

You have to stand through it all. Trust and believe that God is with you. That He is willing and able to get you through. Be confident in knowing that if there is an attack on this end, it's usually because there is a breakthrough coming right around the corner on the other end. My wonderful mother continually shared words of wisdom with me while I was going through my storm at work. She told me, "While it might feel like your heart was ripped open and like there was no way you could bear it yet one more minute, be encouraged, sweety," she said. "Know that this ordeal will not last always. It too shall pass."

As I have had to learn, I need for you to know this as well. The storm is only for a little while. God has already provided you with the strength you need to endure. Stand! You have believed. You have exercised your faith, you have already demonstrated your faith by giving, and you have already put a plan together. Now stand! Stand in faith.

Yes, this is the time the devil will attempt to release all that he has to tear you down. Yes, he will attempt to do away with all that was done by your believing, by your having faith, by your giving, and by your creating a plan. Yes, your months and months, years and years of sacrifice, praying, planning, and believing could be wiped away with one swift and quick blow, but only if you allow it. So don't allow it.

The enemy, in haste and in desperation, is trying his darndest to fight to stay alive. He's falling and he's going down, but he's going kicking and screaming and looking for someone who he can try and drag down with him. You must stand. Rise to your feet, remain motionless, take a position, and remain firm and steadfast. Exodus 14:13 says, "And Moses said to the people, 'Do not be afraid. Stand still, and see the salvation of the Lord, which He will accomplish for you today.'"

You can see from what I have shared with you how the devil can try to destroy you. His attack is specific and targeted. The other interesting thing that I just want to share with you is that right before I went through my storm, I had just decided to recommit my entire life to Christ. I committed to give Him my talent, my time, and my treasure.

I just woke up one morning and purposed in my heart that everything I do and say from that point going forward would be Christ centered. And when I did make that declarative statement, it was almost as if the devil had been pushed off the cliff and was about to fall a horrible fall. But he was trying not to go down without a fight, so he tried to bring me down with him. Well, no . . . no . . . no. Not gonna happen. It took just a bit of time, a real hard gut check, and a blow to my spirit but I refused. I declared that despite what things look like, despite what my situation says, I know that God's Word is true.

I am more than a conqueror; there is nothing too hard for God; I can do all things through Christ Jesus who strengthens me. Greater is He who is in me than He who is in the world. All things work according to the will of my Lord. This is not my battle to fight. It is a fight or rather a war against principalities.

Therefore, it was not necessary for me to not only join the battle but not necessary for me to fear as well. God will provide. God is my protector, my rock, my shield, and my provider. I recognized that I needed the strength to stand, so I found it in God.

We Find Strength To Stand When We Pray

Okay, so now that you know that right before you receive your breakthrough, a storm is subject to come your way. And although it may not look exactly like mine, it is a storm nonetheless. You have read and understood from earlier chapters that you have to, in fact, stand. Let's make sure that you know how to stand.

Standing requires strength. We need to be bold enough and courageous enough to stand. One way we get that boldness and courage is with prayer. I recognize that prayer is not easy for some people to do. As a matter of fact, some people say that they are turned off when they hear others talk about prayer. It is possible they are turned off because they think prayer is a substitute for taking action. But that is simply not the case. Prayer is action. Prayer gives new believers and veteran believers the courage to act. Others might shy away from prayer because they believe that prayer must sound like reading the King James version of the Bible—you know, with the "thou sayest" and "ye maketh" and such. They think they are not sophisticated enough to pray that way. So they decide not to pray at all. Prayer does not have to be that way. As a matter of fact, prayer can be approached as a simple conversation with God. My personal opinion about prayer is that I believe God cares more about the fact that the prayer is coming from our hearts and a pure desire to commune with Him versus whether we have the "thou's" in the right place.

I personally shied away from prayer for quite some time in my life. It wasn't because I just didn't want to spend time talking to God. I really did want to spend time with God. My fear was that God would not hear my prayer because I didn't know how to pray. I was under the impression that unless I prayed in a very specific way for a very specific time, God would not hear nor answer my prayer. And using that rationale, I honestly believed that there was a specific prayer formula that needed to be followed. Similar to those who thought prayer needed to sound like the King James version of the Bible, I thought the prayer formula was one where I had to have just the right amount of "therefores" and "thus sayeths" all in the right place and used at just the right time. I also thought that in order for God to hear my prayer, I needed to reference several scriptures in my prayer. And not just reference the scriptures but that I also needed to know them by heart, sort of like a recitation. That meant that I would have to memorize them and include them in my prayer.

The other item that made up my prayer "formula" during that time was the duration of my prayer. I thought that when I prayed, it had to be at least an hour long. And there was no way that I could have that much conversation for God at that time in my life, especially if I had to use the formula I just mentioned. I couldn't even fathom what I could say to God for sixty whole minutes. Ay, yah yah. And then, of course, there is the "How do you position your body when you pray" question. And duh, yep, that was included in my self-described "prayer formula" as well. Of course, I thought, I had to pray on my knees. So then the challenge became where I could get on my knees for an hour to pray and how much cushion and padding I had available to ensure I was comfortable.

So there I was, yearning to pray and wanting to pray, but thinking that I had to have all the King James lingo in my head and use them in the right places during the prayer and I had to have at least five or six scriptures memorized and use them in the right places as well. Then I needed to have a stopwatch or a timer around because I had to pray minimally for sixty minutes straight with no interruption and no break in thought, and lastly, I had to do all of this while on my knees. And it was for that reason that I shied away from prayer. Without even knowing it, via my self-prescribed "prayer formula," I created an unreasonably high standard for me to follow. And the impact of that was that I just did not pray at all. I think this happens more often than not with people. I believe we set expectations on ourselves that have nothing or little to do with what God expects from us when we are trying to commune and develop a relationship with Him.

However, once I matured spiritually, it was up to me to find out what God really expected from me in my prayer life. It was up to me to open the Bible and see what the Word of God says about prayer. So when I did finally get a revelation of how to pray, my life changed and just in the nick of time. Praying becomes an important tool to use when we are in the midst of life's challenges. Admittedly, I still don't spend as much time in prayer as I would like to and as I should. But when I do spend time in prayer each day, it is such a powerful and moving experience. I found a new formula for prayer that works for me and allows me to hear from God, and it is amazing.

My prayer time with God is not timed. I place no expectation on myself of exactly how much time I should pray. There isn't a stopwatch around me. The only consistent caveat I place on myself regarding time and prayer is that I want to make sure that I pray as long as it takes for me to share with God what is on my heart at that time or hear from Him regarding a certain situation. If I decided to pray because there is a specific question or concern that I needed guidance on, then the duration of my prayer is for the period of time it takes for me to either hear from God or feel in my spirit that God will direct me along the way. If I have come to God in prayer because I am in the middle of a crisis or a storm and I need to be encouraged, then I spend enough time with the Lord for Him to hear all of my fears, for me to release my cares, and up until the time I obtain strength from His Word to move forward.

The other revelation about prayer that I received is that I do not have to sound like a Biblical scholar in my prayer. It's not the number of scriptures I memorize and use or the King James lingo I incorporate, but rather I can speak with God in ways that sound like a typical conversation I would have with someone I love and respect. Notice, I said like a conversation I have with someone "I love and respect." Whenever we commune with the Lord, it should come from a place of reverence. Reverence means to show respect or fear. I have used several words to describe my feelings about God like awe, obedience, humbling, and love. So when I talk to my heavenly Father, I do so out of the awe of how powerful He is, how humbling it feels to be able to be in His presence, and to know that He loves me, and that as I do so, I commit to be obedient to His will for my life out of complete and utter everlasting love for who He is, what He is, and all that He has done.

Do we have to pray on our knees? I haven't found a scripture in the Bible that says we must pray on our knees. That being said, I have always prayed on my knees. I recall making a vow to God sometime ago that while I still had knees to kneel down on and while I was still physically able to pray on my knees, I would in fact do just that. I made that vow sometime ago, and I believed I have learned a lot about praying and how to pray since I actually made that commitment to God. And although, I often pray on my knees, there are "in the moment" prayers when I do not pray on my knees. For example, if I am driving in my car and I get a phone call that someone else is in a car accident and is in need of prayer, I probably won't pull the car over, get out, and fall on my knees and pray for that person but rather pray right there in the moment for that individual's recovery.

I believe that most people fall to their knees in prayer because it represents humbling yourself out of respect and reverence for the Lord. It is a sign of humility and respect for God. Moses, David, and Joseph, for example, bowed their heads as a sign of reverential respect and humility that is shown to God.

In addition to my being on my knees when I pray and having conversation with God from my heart, I also make sure that when I pray, I try to find a private, isolated space where I can be away from any distractions. The first reason I do this is because I believe that I owe it to God to give Him my undivided attention. The second reason is because I want to make sure that I am focused on Him as well, especially when it is wisdom or guidance or healing that I need from Him. Additionally, as hard as this really is for me personally, I try to ensure that my personal prayer time is a gadget-free, distraction-free prayer time. I realize that this might sound a little weird to some, but believe it or not, there are folks whose gadgets are attached to their hips. They won't make a move without their laptops, iPads, Kindles, iPhones, Droids, Sidekicks, 72-inch TV with the universal remote, and any other electronic-type devices. So yes, I am a firm believer that prayer time should be gadget-free—distraction-free. Yes, your Facebook update and your next Tweet will just have to wait. Try to spend some quality alone time with God without the distractions.

When I am in prayer, I focus on the quality of prayer not on the quantity of prayer time. I would rather spend twenty revelation-filled minutes with God than an hour of rehearsed prayer or scripture. Now this might not be the case for everyone, but this is the formula that worked for me as I matured spiritually in my walk with God and continually draw closer to Him daily. I am at a much different place now with my own spiritual walk with God, so I actually have had many power-packed, spirit-filled, hour-long prayers with my Father.

Stand Using The Right Prayer Formula

When we make prayer part of our life's routine, the impact it has on us is truly amazing. It creates an opportunity and a vehicle for us to communicate with God. The more we communicate with God, the freer we feel and the freer we become. Taking the time to kneel down in prayer, away from the hustle and bustle of day-to-day life, enables us to share with God all the things in our hearts and in our minds. It allows us to take God at His Word. We truly have an opportunity to cast all of our cares on Him. The more we cast, the freer we become and the less burdensome we become.

My newfound prayer formula that I shared with you above has enabled me to do just that. It has enabled me to cast all of my cares on the Lord. Somehow the saying that "my burdens have been lifted" doesn't even do it justice. It feels as though I am light as a feather. All the heaviness is gone—no worry and no stress. It is as if the problem no longer exists. I truly feel free. And it is that freedom that gives me strength. I feel myself becoming physically and spiritually stronger, almost like there is nothing or no one that can hinder me, stop me, or get in my way. And the stronger I feel, the bolder and more confident I become. Sometimes I get to a point where I actually dare a problem to come my way like "Hit me with your best shot,." With all that I have been through, with all that I have persevered through, and with the strength and might that I have gained knowing that God hears and answers my prayers, I am literally "unhindered and untouched" by any force. With God at my side, who can come against me?

The strength and the courage I am able to obtain and maintain through a consistent prayer life is awesome. And not only does it allow me to cast my care, free myself of the burden, and build strength in my spirit, but I also get to actually communicate with God. The more I humble myself before Him with an open heart and mind in prayer, the more I am able to position myself to hear directly from Him. When I am still, quiet, and focused in prayer, I position myself to hear directly from God. As you consider your own prayer formula, an additional tool for learning how to pray is a book called "Teach Me to Pray" by D. Qwynn Gross.

In my early days, I often imagined God speaking to me in a loud thunderous voice that shook the house and rocked the neighboring trees—you know, that deep baritone voice of like James Earl Jones or someone like that. I think I might have been watching too many media-portrayed voices of God. I was looking for God to speak to me with a voice from the outside.

But what I have recently learned is that God dwells on the inside of us and He will speak to us through us. Now don't get me wrong. I'm not saying that God never speaks to anyone from an outside voice. God is God. He can do what He wants, including speaking to one of His children using the voice He wants, as loud as He wants, and when He wants. I am just saying that my experiences of hearing God speak to me have been soft voices that resonate from inside of me, almost like through my spirit versus through my outer ear.

Nevertheless, hearing from God is simply awesome. A continuous prayer life will give you just that—freedom, strength, courage, and a word directly from the Lord. All of those things are what you need to stand in the midst of the storm.

Stand Using Meditation:
If You Ever Worried, You Know How To Meditate

Once you are able to get strength from prayer while you stand, you need to maintain that strength. It might sound funny but you need to strengthen that strength. You can do that through meditation. We gain and maintain strength by meditating on the Word of God. We seem to talk a lot more about meditation these days than we have in the past. More often than not, we typically hear the term meditate associated with a non-Biblical-based activity, such as Yoga. And it's amazing how many folks understand the concept of meditating if associated with Yoga versus understanding meditating as it relates to the Bible. I don't have anything in particular against the activity of Yoga, but I just want to help you understand how to meditate on God's word, which will help give you strength to stand.

The word meditate means to think deeply or focus one's mind for a period of time for religious or spiritual purposes or as a method of relaxation. It's the latter part of this definition that most folks associate the act of meditation. Most think of it as a method of relaxation. And somehow, I think that they think meditation associated with the Word of God is far from relaxing. It really does not have to be that way.

Meditating on the Word of God can be as relaxing as taking the scripture Jeremiah 29:11 and replaying it over and over again in your mind. This scripture says, "'For I know the plans I have for you,' declares the Lord, 'plans to prosper you and not harm you, plans to give you hope and a future" (NIV). So what happens when you read this scripture and begin to think about it over and over again? I am sure that it will not only relax you, but it will encourage you as well. It will give you a sense of security knowing that God has plans for you. It will give you a sense of relief knowing that God has no plans to harm you and will give you a sense of warmth on the inside knowing that God has plans to give you hope and a future. Meditating on the Word of God is inspiring, motivating, and encouraging. And yes, it can be relaxing as well. The Word of God tells us over and over again that we do not have to live defeated lives. We do not have to live lives of hopelessness or despair. As a matter of fact, if we just stick with the scripture Jeremiah 29:11, we know that God has plans to give us hope and a future. God has plans to prosper us. So "Why then do we find it so hard to "meditate" and replay this scripture over and over in our mind?" is a really good question. Perhaps it is because we believe we have to treat meditation as a highly religious activity performed by only the spiritually mature. That is not true. We all can meditate anywhere and anytime. What's most important is what we meditate on. The answer to that is we should unequivocally meditate on the Word of God.

I personally believe that each and every one of us meditates at some point of the day, each and every day. There are things that we play over and over again in our minds on a daily basis. It could be related to work. Maybe a meeting didn't go well because you gave the wrong answer when the boss asked you a question. And now that it is all over and done, you still can't get that question and your silly answer out of your mind. You replay it in your head over and over again in your mind. Maybe it's about a problem that you are having with your kids. And you are not sure what to do or who to turn to, but you continue to think about that problem over and over again all day. Perhaps it is about a failed marriage or a business you started that has been in the red for the last year and you don't know what to do. If you have been focused on and thinking about your problems over and over again, you are participating in a form of meditation. The world gives it another name. They call it worrying.

Well, if you can worry, you know how to meditate. Although there's really no good time to worry, I think the worst time that we should spend any time worrying is when we are in the midst of a storm. How can we obtain the strength and the courage to stand when in the midst of the storm if all we can focus on is that we are fact in the midst of the storm? Stop thinking of the storm that you are in but rather see beyond the storm. Beyond the storm is Jeremiah 29:11. Beyond the storm is Philippians 1:6: "He who began a good work in you will continue until the day of Jesus Christ." Beyond the storm is Isaiah 40:31: "Those who wait on the Lord shall renew their strength; they shall mount up with wings like eagles, they shall run and not be weary, they shall walk and not faint." Beyond the storm is James 4:6-8: "He gives more grace . . . Therefore submit to God. Resist the devil and he will flee from you."

Meditate On The Word Of God

Some of you might be thinking that this is easier said than done. You might not even know where to start or how to find a scripture to mediate on. That is a good question. For those of us who have never meditated on the Word of God, we would in fact need help identifying the right scriptures to meditate on while in the midst of the storm.

There are several books that I can quickly refer you to for the answer. But I'll start with the most important one, the Bible. The Bible is filled with lots of awesome promises of God that give us courage and strength when we need. But if we don't pick up the Bible, we won't even know that those promises exist, let alone identify a scripture for meditation. So I say, start by just picking up the Bible, opening it up, and reading it.

And because of technology, it's very easy to have access to the Bible in various forms. You can purchase a Bible from a book store. You can download an electronic copy of the Bible on an e-reader device. You can even download an audio version of the Bible on your iPod or MP3 player. While I encourage everyone to start by actually "reading" the pages of the Bible, I am reminded that given the times we are living in, the convenience of technology is astounding. So go ahead, plug in your iPod or MP3 player and upload the Bible. Read the Word, listen to the Word, and meditate on the Word.

Similar to the private time that we discussed earlier when you pray, I encourage you to have that same type of quiet time when you are reading the Bible and meditating on the Word of God. And just in case there was the slight possibility that you might have forgotten what the quiet time meant, it means that during this time, as you read or listen to the Bible, you will need to put your cell away for a second, shut off the computer, and try to stop your fingers from wanting to text someone every two seconds. Find a quite location, bring your Bible or your iPod (with the Bible on it), and begin to read and listen. And as you read and reread the scriptures, focus deeply on them, let them sink into your mind, and begin hearing your own voice utter the words of the scripture. Replay it over and over in your head until it seeps into your spirit—until it is able to wipe away whatever else has happened or will happen during the course of the day.

When we spend our time filling our minds and spirit with what the Word of God says, the less time we spend filling it with what the five o'clock news says. Let's have more control over what we think about and meditate on. If we take a minute to just think about it, what would we find we spend our time meditating on? We might be able to find the answer to that question by asking just a couple more questions like "What do you spend your time reading?" and "What are you spending your time watching?" Or maybe the right question is "Who do you spend your time listening to?" The answers to those questions actually become what we tend to create as the subject of our daily meditation.

And if we surround ourselves with people who constantly whisper in our ears that the economy is about to collapse—that it is going to be really, really bad—that might be the subject of our meditation for that day. If we surround ourselves with people who do nothing but gossip, complain, and have nothing but negative things to say all day, perhaps that becomes what we end up meditating on for that day. Even our own thoughts and words can create the subject of our meditation. If we spend our time telling ourselves how tired we are or how sick we are, then that becomes the subject of our meditation. And it's the tired, sick, broke thought that replays over and over again in our mind and thoughts. When that happens, it is difficult enough to deal with day-to-day challenges, let alone being able to stand when we are under attack by the enemy.

In order to stand through the storm, you need to draw strength from the Word of God. In order to stand through the storm, you have to have something within you that says that no weapon formed against me shall prosper. Something within you that says, "I am above and not below. I am more than a conqueror," and that "I can do all things through Christ Jesus who strengthens me." Because when you have those words—those words of power—no matter what the world hits you with, you will be able to endure. If life hits you with all it's got—the worst of the worst of times—meditating on God's

Word enables you to shake it off because you have a bounce back in your spirit like water rolling off of a duck's back. You can declare that you are blessed and highly favored and that you have the victory despite what it may look like. That's what it means to stand. That is how you can stand if you have the strength, and the spiritual weapons that come from meditating on the Word of God. So instead of meditating on what's on TV every Wednesday at 5:00 p.m. or your favorite non-Christian/gospel song all day long or the news that just repeats itself every four hours, why don't you meditate on the Word of God? Feed on the Word of God. Read the Bible, re-read the Bible. Meditate on the Word. Study it. Focus on it.

If we just replace those things that we tend to consistently worry about each day with a scripture (the Word of God) and we think on those things, that type of meditation builds our spirits and draws us closer to God. And it will strengthen us, giving us courage and the might we need to stand in the midst of the storm.

Stand By Confessing God's Word

The next thing that you need to do to overcome the storm and experience breakthrough is confess. Meditating on the Word helps to build your faith and strengthen your spirit. It creates a bounce back in your spirit that you need to get back up again when you've been attacked. When you add confession of the Word to your praying and meditating, you take it to a whole other level.

It's the confession that declares victory over your entire spirit. And where you have declared victory, meditated on victory, and confessed victory, doubting that you will be victorious isn't even an option. You know you are confessing the Word of God when you can look at your bank account and see that there is not enough in it to pay your rent, to pay your mortgage, and to put gas in your car to get to and fro to work for the rest of the week, but nevertheless, you look at your account and declare that all your needs are met according to his riches in glory (Philippians 4:19). It is confessing the Word of God when you can look at a bare food cupboard in the kitchen and say that you have more than enough. This is what confessing the Word can do for you.

Confessing the Word is really just a natural transition for you during your meditation time. As you meditate on the Word, you begin to identify scriptures that just resonates in your spirit. They are relevant to what you are going through. And because that particular scripture has meaning for you, you tend to remember it more than the others. And because you remember it, it now just comes to mind for you when you are in the middle of the test. When it comes to mind, say it out loud. Then say it out loud again. Now you are confessing the Word of God. Use that same scripture again but a little louder and then louder still until your confession manifests itself into a loud, confident boldness that shakes the spirit and causes the angels of heaven to act on your behalf. It is confessing the Word of God that causes someone at your job or in the bank, or one of your friends to use their power, influence, and ability to help you prosper. Confessing the Word of God pierces the veil of doubt, fear, and insecurity. Then it looks to destroy it utterly and completely.

Similar to belief, confessing is an action word. It means that you have to do something. You have to act. First, you need something to confess; you need God's words to speak. As we learned in the previous sections, we get that when we meditate on the Word. When you read passages of the Bible over and over, you make a scriptural deposit into your spirit. And it is this scriptural deposit that will surface as you are being challenged by the rough times that come with living in the world. Know that you can combat the attack. You can combat the attack by confessing the Word of God. And as you use your confession to build your strength, you stand up boldly, confidently, and declare with conviction that you are an overcomer.

Last night, I pulled up my bank account on line. I had $121, and I knew that I would not be getting paid for another week and a half, yet I needed about $120 to purchase bus tickets in order to get back and forth to work. I needed to pay one of my smaller school loans, and December's mortgage had not been paid yet either. Given what I saw in my bank account, I have to know enough not to trust what I see but believe God for things that I do not see. And what I do see is that all my needs are met according to God's riches in glory. What I do see is that I have more than enough. I confess that the funds in my bank account are in abundance, to the full, and to the overflow and that not only is there enough to cover December's mortgage, but there is also enough for January, February, and March. That is my confession.

Those are the only words that I will allow out of my mouth during these times, not that there isn't enough to cover my expenses or that I don't have any money. Please understand that our words have power and we are able to speak life to our words. If you say you do not have enough, then you don't and you won't have enough. If you say that you will never get a job, then you might not. If you say that you are always sick, then guess what?—you are opening yourself up for perpetual sickness. What you confess is what you are declaring over your life and over your situation. And how is one strong enough, confident enough, and bold enough to stand if the confessions from their mouth are contrary to their posturing, contrary to their prayers, and contrary to what they read and see in the Bible.

Pray, meditate, and confess God's blessings over your life. As a matter of fact, tell God, "God, You can trust me with money, and not only can you trust me with money to manage all of my finances with diligence and obedience, but you can also trust me to use the money you give me to bless others." Tell God He can trust you in your marriage and that you will honor the person whom He has placed in your life. Tell God He can trust you with the vessel He has allowed you to dwell in for these years and you declare your body a healthy body. Declare these things, confess these things, and you will see yourself not only standing in the midst of the storm but you will also see beyond the storm, out of the storm, above the storm, and into your breakthrough.

Hah! Your confession, your meditation, and your prayer is a success. You are out of what you were in, and you have encountered a boundlessness that you have never experienced before. You have a sense of peace about you that brings calm in the midst of the deadliest storm. You did it. You were able to stand. And that's it. Now go and tell someone else how to do it. Go share the good news. Let them know what a magnificent God we have. Go tell them that although life will try to bring them down, they need only stand. Just stand still in the midst of the storm and the Lord will deliver you from the circumstance.

Now that you have stood, consider all of the four principles. Using all of them together in sequence or at the same time will put you on and keep you on a path of everlasting and limitless prosperity in every area of your life. At this point, please know that in order to be delivered from any trial, tribulation, or storm that you are experiencing, the principles in this book can help you. Allow God's Word to work in your life. Believe that God is able and His Word is true. Believe that greater is He that is in you than he that is in the world. Act on your belief by exercising the scriptural principle of giving and do so with an unreluctantly and cheerful heart. Give of your time, talent, and resources. Sow a seed in the very area that you lack. Give freely without doubt or fear to someone or something more needy than you, even if you know that throughout it all, you cannot afford to give. Do it in faith and in belief that it will be returned to you hundredfold. Your giving can also be your sowing a seed, a seed against the destruction that is causing you pain and a seed of faith in prosperity—that all of your needs will be met according to His riches and glory.

Then put a plan in place—a plan that keeps you on the path of continued belief in God and a plan that lays out your commitment of tithing faithfully, giving unconditional love offerings to those or anyone in need, and a plan that reminds you to stand in the midst of the storm. This becomes your reference tool that you can look back on in the event that there is a moment of weakness, doubt, or fear. Put a plan in place to break through the strongholds in your life no matter what they might be. And when your plan is in place, you get up, roll your shoulders back, pick your chin up, hold your head up high, and stand.

Stand In Expectation

Stand in expectation. Know that all of the work you put into believing, giving, planning, and standing will be honored by God. Stand in expectation. Expect to see the fruit of your labor. Expect to reap what you have sowed. Expect to see and live the change in your life that you have believed God for.

Your breakthrough is imminent. Don't stop now. Do not faint in well doing. But expect to actually see and live the very thing that you have been believing God for. Expect and prepare for it to come to fruition. To carry this thing out to the very end, you must remain steadfast in your belief. Whatever it is that you said that you want or need God to do for you when you started this journey, hold on to that. Do not get all the way to this point to give up now. You must expect that it will in fact happen. You have to expect it the same way that you expect some things to happen in the natural.

For example, let's say you have a headache and you run to take an aspirin. You are actually taking that aspirin with the expectation that it will actually get rid of your headache, right? I'm sure that as soon as you popped the aspirin in your mouth, you did not expect your headache to disappear right that very moment, did you? No, you understand and expect for the aspirin to take some time before it works through your system to get rid of the headache. On some occasions, if it didn't work fast enough, you might even have expected that taking another two aspirins will really do the trick.

Nevertheless and no matter what it is we expect, in the natural, we expect the thing to happen as a result of us taking some type of action. For example, when we put gas in the car, we expect for the car to drive as far and as long as the number of miles listed on the dashboard. When we go to work and clock in for our eight-hour day, we expect to be paid for that eight-hour day. In the natural and in the world, we understand that if we have an expectation and we act on that expectation, we really expect for that thing to come to fruition. We expect for it to become a reality.

The same holds true for us when we operate according to the principles of the Word of God. When we set out to live our lives according to God's Word, we can expect something to happen in our lives. We can expect our lives to change. And if you really stop to think about it, how much more faith should we have in our gas tank, our employer, or that aspirin we took than in God, the one who created the heavens and the earth? So now that you have made a determination in your life to break through the strongholds in your life by believing, giving, planning, and standing, you must be equally, if not more, convinced that you can expect God to show up and show out in your life.

Expect complete health and healing over your life and your family's lives. Expect to get that new job at that specific location for that specific salary you have prayed for. Expect to overcome your financial struggles and cancel all debts in your life. Expect to be healed from the hurt and the pain of your past so that you can break through to your new future. Expect that you can put the pieces back together in your marriage and you can live a happy life with a healthy family structure. Expect that you can go and start that new business that you believe God has birthed in you, and expect that it will be successful. Expect that you can experience victory in every area of your life. Expect that you can live a life of love, joy, peace, and prosperity. Expect!

CHAPTER 5:

Break Through to Your Breakthrough!

God's Timing, Not Ours

A nd while you stand in expectation, do not be weary in well doing (Galatians 6:9). Keep pushing through. It might not all happen the very hour, minute, and second that you wanted it to, but it does not mean it will not happen. It will happen. And it will happen with God's timing, not ours. Just because it did not happen the exact moment that you wanted it to happen, it does not mean that it won't happen at all. To the contrary, it will happen. You have to be just as convinced and determined as ever to believe that it will. You have come too far to give up now. So don't let you get in your own way of experiencing your breakthrough.

Sometimes I really do think that we become the barriers to our own success and our own victory. It is almost as if we decided to run a marathon. We trained for the marathon. We went out and bought new sneakers for it. We changed our eating habits and have become physically fit, and we are ready. And here we are on the day of the race. We know that it will be a five-mile run, and we head out to the starting line ready to go the distance. We start the race, and we are running strong and with great form at a smart pace. One mile into the five-mile stretch, it begins to rain. It is just a steady drizzle; the ground gets a bit wet and slippery, but we can handle it. Now we are two miles into the five-mile stretch, and the drizzle turns into a heavy downpour so much so that it impacts our stride and the stride of the other runners as well. Several runners drop out of the race. So now we have a decision to make. Do we dig in and keep going, or do we pull out?

Well, we think about it for a second and we say to ourselves, We've trained for this marathon, and we have trained in rainy conditions. Admittedly, we have trained in rain but nothing as heavy as this. Nevertheless, we say to ourselves, "We can handle it," so we decide to dig in and push through. We run on and here we are now four miles into the five-mile stretch. It is a straightaway so we can see the crowd cheering ahead of us. The finish line ribbon is visible in the distance. We are almost there. We can taste it. But sure enough, the last stretch gets even tougher because the wind has just kicked in, and it kicks in strong. It begins to throw the heavy raindrops across our faces and into our eyes.

You feel yourself slowing down, your vision is slightly impaired, and you can no longer see the cheering crowd clearly in front of you. The last mile stretch is starting to feel like five miles all over again because you now have to run against the strong wind current. What do you do? You are almost there. You expected to win this race, but you were not quite prepared for the weather conditions. Do you give up right when you are closest to the finish line than you have ever been before? You are only 250 feet away from the finish line. What do you do? Do you give up?

Some of you reading this are probably saying to yourself, "No way, of course you don't give up when you are right at the finish line." Well, the same holds true for you. You have come so far. Why would you give up now? You owe it to yourself to win the marathon. You owe it to yourself to experience the breakthrough that you have been asking for, praying for, and believing God for. Why give up now? Do not let a little rain throw you off course. Do not let some little thing throw you off course. And just because you haven't received your breakthrough the second you thought you should have received it doesn't mean you won't receive it. So don't let that throw you off course either.

God knows what you need and when you need it. As a matter of fact, before you even started this journey—before you even picked up this book to read it—God knew that you would. He knows what's in your heart, He knows the pain that you are facing, and He knew what you needed before you even asked for it. He also knows the exact moment you will receive the breakthrough in your life. So faint not. Do not be weary in well doing (Galatians 6:9). It will happen, it already is happening, and you might just not know it yet.

It's Happening

Celebrate how far you have come. Take a moment to recognize where you were and where you are now. As I have been writing this book to you for our breakthrough, there have been times where I have been frustrated. I was not seeing the breakthrough that I thought that I would see at this point in my own breakthrough journey. I thought that my breakthrough should have flashed before my very eyes like a big cloud of smoke or a bright beaming light. I wanted the miracle of breakthrough to just drop out of the sky and land on me like in the movies.

How silly of me to think that way. I was looking in the wrong place. What about you, are you looking in the wrong place too? For those of you who know for a fact that you have received your breakthrough since you picked up this book and started your journey, that is awesome—truly awesome. Rejoice and share your experience with others. Let them know exactly what God has done for you and in you.

For those of you who are still expecting it, do not get frustrated the way that I did. And be sure not to look in the wrong place the way that I did. What I discovered was that my breakthrough starts with me. It begins from inside of me. It is coming from within me. I learned that the way that I think, the way that I believe, and the way that I pray is completely different now than they were when I was starting to write to you. I see things with a totally different lens now than I did earlier. My approach to handling day-to-day challenges is different. I am more optimistic about how I believe things will turn out. I feel confident that things in my life will only get better. There is now a sense of boldness about me that had not existed before and certainly had not existed prior to writing this book. What I discovered is that my life has changed. The insecurities and the fears that I had before I started this journey are gone. I have newfound wisdom that I now use to make decisions. I feel freer than I had prior to starting the journey. And what God revealed to me was that this was in fact the breakthrough I needed. It starts from within me. It starts with me.

So ask yourself, what is different about you now? Has anything changed since you began your journey? If so, take a second, grab a pen and piece of paper, and write it down. Go ahead and list those things that have changed since you started this journey. No matter what it is, write it all out. Is it the way you pray or the way you approach day-to-day challenges? Is it the way you think or the decisions that you make? Are you happier or healthier? Whatever it is, take a second to write it all down. No matter what that list looks like, chances are the words on that list say that your life has changed. And isn't that what you wanted before you picked up this book? Isn't that what you said you needed as you read the chapter on believing? Wasn't it you who said that you wanted and needed your life to change? Well, change is what you wanted and change is what you received.

Rejoice! The change that has taken place within you is in fact part of your breakthrough. Celebrate! It is happening right this very moment. It is happening. Celebrate, laugh, and/or cry. Testify if you must, but do whatever it takes for you to recognize and celebrate that you are living your breakthrough right this very moment. Now go and share that with someone else who you know is also expecting a breakthrough in their life.

This is just the tip of the iceberg. It is only part of your breakthrough. God has so much more in store for you. Do not stop believing. Do not stop giving. Do not stop planning, and do not stop standing. There is more in store just for you. You are destined for greatness.

CONCLUSION:

MY TESTIMONY

My dear, dear reader, I mentioned to you that I would be writing this book encouraging you to break through while I encourage myself. All throughout the chapters, I have shared testimonies of things that have happened to me in the past, but mostly I have been sharing things that have happened to me as I actually have been going through them while writing this literary work. And (sigh) what a journey it has been. I started off this book by telling you that I was believing God for total and complete debt cancellation in my life.

I shared with you that I currently have approximately $600,000 worth of debt. I shared my income-to-debt ratio with you, talked a little bit about my expenses, etc. I also told you that not only was I expecting God to cancel all of the debt in my life, but I also mentioned to you that I was also expecting Him to bless my family in such a way that I would no longer have family dependents depending on my income to support them. That means that as the Lord was performing this miracle of debt cancellation in my life, He was also positioning my family for financial breakthrough and blessings in their lives as well—that they would be blessed in such a way that they would not only become self-sufficient but be in a position to be able to bless others in need.

Throughout this work, I remained hopeful that God would turn my situation around. And even while writing the book, I have seen my situation go from worse to better to worse and better again. There have been times during these months of writing where I have experienced a drop in my credit score, returned checks, and insufficient fund fees. I have experienced the continued challenges that people go through as they so desperately attempt to pull themselves out of a financial rut. I prayed and prayed for God to turn my mortgage situation around. Remember, I paid approximately 3.5 percent more interest than the average home owner. And you know that even one percent reduction in the interest rate can save the homeowner tens of thousands of dollars in their mortgage.

My point is that this quest is ongoing. I have not just prayed to God once for Him to refinance my mortgage at a low rate, give jobs to my family members without work, give me financial wisdom so that I may exercise the diligence in my finances that I need in order to pull myself out of debt. It is not just about praying for this one time and that is it. No, this is an ongoing quest and faith fight that I must stay in despite what it looks like. So I have continued to meditate on God's Word, I have fasted continually, and I have changed my spending habits. I have operated under the principles of sowing and reaping. I have given generously and cheerfully to others in the need. And I have not done these things as a one-time event. I have been doing these things continually through this journey. And I have done so still believing that God would deliver me from all that which I asked for Him to deliver me from. I have been following the same ideas and principles that I have shared with you in this book.

In addition to my financial challenges, I have also shared with you the painful trials that I faced at my job—how painful it was for me and the impact that it had on my life. So here I am, nearing the end of this literary work and I am unable to see (with my natural eyes) where the complete debt cancellation will come from or see how God will make a way for financial freedom for my family. Here I am, after having given you the framework and the plan to pull yourself out of your situation by believing, by giving, by planning, and by standing, I stand, doing the same thing.

While I wanted to be in a much different place as I neared the end of writing this book, it is now fantastically clearer to me just how far I have come. I am happier now than I have ever been in my life, not because God has wiped away all of my debt (as I am not completely there yet), not because I no longer face challenges at the job (there are still a few left), and not because my family no longer is financially dependent on me, for none of those things are completely true. I still have debt; I still face challenges at work. My family still experience challenges in their finances, and they rely on me to help them.

Nevertheless, I am happier now than I have ever been in my life because through this journey, I have strengthened my relationship with God. I have gained wisdom and a sense of boldness and security that I can't even describe. I am happier now than I have ever been in my life because I now know the plan He has for my life. I know what He wants for me and what He wants to do through me. And this literary work and my ability to share this with you is just part of it. I have a newfound perspective on life. I can see things about me and others that I was blinded to before. My newfound perspective on life allows me to see and change those things that at one time or another, would have appeared to have been mountains and are in reality little mo hills.

I have a newfound boldness in life—one where I am now confident that my financial situation is temporary. I know that my family's situation is temporary. I know that I will not always be in debt because my being in debt is contrary to God's plan for my life. My new perspective in life revealed to me that the breakthrough that I was expecting to fall on me starts from within me. And yes, I am now free. I have been and am continuing to be released from the heaviness of debt and the heaviness of insecurity and fear. I have been and am continuing to be released from the heaviness of doubt.

You see, through writing this book, I have broken through those barriers, limitations, stresses, and fears that held me captive for so long. Breaking through those things has enabled me to experience life differently. I laugh more and I smile more. I love harder, I live harder, and I give harder and live life on purpose and with a purpose. I broke through to my breakthrough and am living it even now with every word I type. Hallelujah!

And that's not all. God has allowed for some of the things in the natural to change for me as well. God did make a way for me to refinance our home. I was able to save a significant amount of money from my mortgage payment because of it. He has allowed for me to receive a financial increase through several different resources. My credit score has gone up. I am also healthier now than I was before. My energy is now at a point where it is supposed to be for someone my age. I now can honestly say that I love my job. I went from working at a place where I experienced the second hardest thing I have dealt with in my life to now loving my job. And all of that—everything I just shared with you—is breakthrough!

MY PRAYER FOR YOU,

THE READER OF THIS BOOK

Heavenly Father, I humbly ask that You lift up our eyes to see not what stands in front of us but to see the things that cannot be seen with the natural eye. I thank You, Father, that our believing, giving, planning, standing, praying, confessing and fasting have not been in vain. I thank You, Father, that you create a testimony in us that may be shared with the world to encourage them during the most sensitive and challenging times in their lives. Father, we believe in You, we believe You that Your words are true. We believe that You are not a man and You cannot lie. We believe You have plans for our lives, that You have a purpose specifically carved out just for us, and that you have given us all that we need to operate in your purpose for our lives. We believe that we are destined for greatness. We thank You, Lord, for loving us despite and in spite of us. We thank you for the breakthrough in every area of our lives.

In Jesus' name, amen.